DISCARD

DATE DUE

BRODART, CO.

Cat. No. 23-221-003

CHEAP

Cheap is the result of a special collaboration between Kogan Page and Redline Wirtschaft, Germany's leading business publisher. Selected best-selling titles previously published by Redline Wirtschaft are translated into English and published by Kogan Page to ensure a worldwide distribution.

CHEAP

THE **REAL** COST OF THE GLOBAL TREND FOR BARGAINS, DISCOUNTS & CONSUMER CHOICE

DAVID BOSSHART

**KOGAN
PAGE**

London and Philadelphia

Publisher's note
Every possible effort has been made to ensure that the information contained in this book is accurate at the time of going to press, and the publishers and authors cannot accept responsibility for any errors or omissions, however caused. No responsibility for loss or damage occasioned to any person acting, or refraining from action, as a result of the material in this publication can be accepted by the editor, the publisher or any of the authors.

First published in Germany in 2004 by Redline Wirtschaft as *Billig: Wie die Lust am Discount Wirtschaft und Gesellschaft verändert*

First published in Great Britain and the United States in 2006 by Kogan Page Limited

120 Pentonville Road   525 South 4th Street, #241
London N1 9JN   Philadelphia PA 19147
United Kingdom   USA
www.kogan-page.co.uk

© Wirtschaftsverlag Carl Ueberreuter, 2004, 2006

The right of David Bosshart to be identified as the author of this work has been asserted by him in accordance with the Copyright, Designs and Patents Act 1988.

ISBN 0 7494 4534 3

British Library Cataloguing-in-Publication Data

A CIP record for this book is available from the British Library.

Library of Congress Cataloging-in-Publication Data

Bosshart, David.
  [Billig. English]
  Cheap : the real cost of the global trend for bargains, discounts & customer choice / David Bosshart.
    p. cm.

ACC Library Services
Austin, Texas

Iarketing. 5. Globalization.

H
3

Typeset by Saxon Graphics Ltd, Derby
Printed and bound in Great Britain by Creative Print and Design (Wales), Ebbw Vale

Contents

1 The Age of Cheap

Why (almost) everything is getting cheaper

Consumer democracy is the gasoline for the bulldozer of globalization.[1]

'Cheap' is the most important development on our way to the next stage in the modernization process taking place in our economy and our society. Cheap doesn't simply mean 'cheap' – it's about the fundamental attitude people adopt in an age in which everything you can buy is immediately available. It is a logical and significant consequence of developments in already saturated markets that we are concerned today predominantly with topics related to discounting and bargain hunting. It is safe to assume that, in years to come, price is going to play an even more dominant role – when we go shopping, in politics, in morals, within the family, in education and professional training and in our leisure time. Success is a matter of popularity and prominence, while everything else – such as privilege or tradition – takes a back seat. And the most popular and prominent thing in a mature, fully developed market economy is price.

Why the trend towards low-priced goods is changing our lives: the link between prosperity, democracy and price orientation

Discounting is becoming the most important and definitive way of life, and this legitimates new behavioural trends:

- A new modesty transforms parsimony into a desirable property.
- As people become poorer, there is an increased demand for low-priced products.
- Cheap is cool!
- If you pay too much, you're a fool.

In other words, we now unashamedly flaunt attitudes that would once have been frowned upon. We are in the process of becoming a cheap society.

So from the point of view of suppliers, the questions are: 1) Who's better? 2) Who's the cheapest among the best? 3) Who will win the race against time? In other words: Who is fastest off the mark? This is the process of modernization we can expect as markets become freer. And for the customer, this means lower prices.

At this stage in the process of democratization of markets, the question of what came first, supply or demand, is moot. But one thing seems certain: the discount phenomenon is here to stay, irrespective of changes in the economic climate. We have triggered a spiralling development that is not easy to stop. Lower prices mean lower wages. Lower wages mean lower prices. The dangerous game between the desire for goods at discount prices and frustration with the discount trend has begun, and it will produce a domino effect that will change our economies and our society permanently and modernize them in an undreamt-of way.

In recent years, we have heard a lot about globalization and, in the post-new-economy recession years of 2001 to 2003, even more about de-globalization. At the beginning of 2003, the Ahold scandal with its all-too-creative accounting techniques shook us, seemingly confirming our worst suspicions after the stock market hype and the exaggerated developments in the telecommunications industry. But de-globalization would mean reversing the trend we have set in motion, a return to the so-called 'good old days' of nationally oriented economies. Let's not fool ourselves here. Every megatrend has its countertrend. Globalization will continue. There are no signs that it will not, for above all globalization promises one thing: consumer democracy. It promises access to an unbelievable range of goods, so that we will be free to choose and to buy what we really want. It is consumer democracy that really makes everyone equal, independent of class or race. And it comes at lower prices. What reasonable argument could there be against that?

But what is consumer democracy? Consumer democracy is the logical consequence of political democracy. Almost all developed countries today are democracies. Basic human rights are guaranteed; they have become part of a tradition that we no longer have any desire to question because it is taken for granted. It is taken for granted in a positive sense and seen as a given that people can exert political influence by casting their votes in elections. People have learned that this is important, but not all-important. They are clever enough to appreciate these rights, but they are also aware that, in a modern day democracy, political power is exerted indirectly, that it is relatively weak and, above all, that this is a slow process. Today, they are learning that they can exert influence in another way, one that is direct and with immediate effect on their everyday lives, and that this effect can also be of a political nature. In today's consumer democracy, people can cast their vote with their wallets or with plastic money, with their credit cards: I vote for this supplier rather than another. Consumer democracy is never exclusive, it offers options, and people have seen how this gives them more freedom. Nevertheless, they are also getting to know the downside: if you want more freedom, you have to be prepared to assume more personal responsibility. A world that is becoming more and more individualistic as a result of the growing range of goods and services on offer, a world in which our requirements and wishes are more and more sophisticated, can only function if each individual can assume responsibility instead of delegating it to the system.

The more connected our world becomes, the easier it is to gain access to information, the more individuals are required to assume responsibility for arranging their lives and for making the right choices. This means that they can no longer depend on tradition (how did we do things before?). Instead, they have to steer their way through the manifold options offered by global information channels, the trends that arise where networks intersect or simply as a result of the current network constellation. Trends are replacing traditions. This also affects the field of personal risk allocation. Today, we are learning that, in an emergency, we will no longer be able to rely on the state (think about social security), on the company we work for (consider pension funds and the question of returns) or other institutions (eg NGOs), but that we will be responsible for ourselves. If I cannot rely on other sources to cushion the risks, then I have to rely on myself. And that means that today people behave like enterprises whose aim is to maximize profits. This can be easily demonstrated by simply answering the following three questions:

- Would you like to earn more tomorrow than you do today?
- Would you prefer to see lower prices or higher prices when you go shopping?

- If you are one of those privileged enough to be able to put money aside, would you prefer a higher or lower return on your investment?[2]

There is no need for further explanation here; the answers are clear and speak for themselves. I am not (or not any longer) likely to achieve the first aim. I am also not (or not any longer) likely to achieve the third. But the second aim lies well within my grasp. Consumer democracy is about making the fruits of our civilization accessible to larger and larger sections of the population. It has never been so easy to gain access to whatever products and services you desire. This gives us the feeling that it's all out there for the taking. We live in the best of all possible worlds. All we have to do is reach out and take it. Consumer democracy is no more than a gigantic buffet table laden with exquisite dishes to which we all have access, irrespective of class, race or tradition. Thanks to the Age of Cheap, even low-income households can afford champagne and smoked salmon – think of Aldi and Lidl. Freedom as we have come to understand it means that more choice is always better than less choice. Ten TV channels are better than five; 50 are better than 20. And 30 different strawberry yoghurts are better than 20. More than ever before, in consumer democracy the motto is: we are free to do whatever we want. We are free to be whatever we want. We are free to know whatever we want. And above all: we are free to go wherever we want. But the inevitable consequence is that we have to assume more responsibility for ourselves. We have to make our own choices. There is no longer a tradition for us to rely on.

A further consequence of increased access is increased interchange ability. The choice I have is wider – or, to put it negatively, I am forced to spend time continually testing options. Variety can also be troublesome, a stress factor. Where shall I spend my holidays? Shall I go to Ibiza or shall I go back to

Rimini, or is the last-minute offer to Belek perhaps even better? If I don't like organic food, I can buy processed food. And if I'm not happy with the way I look, I can buy skin-care products or go to a plastic surgeon. If I don't like marriage any more, I can choose divorce. If I choose to have children, I will no longer be able to finance the Mercedes coupé. And what is the consequence? The strongest argument of all in mature countries gains more and more weight: the price.

Although prices are relative, they are increasingly important as a means of orientation. The more choice I have, the greater the volatility, the more potential for confusion. Where all products are available and where there are no great differences between them, price is reduced to the question: how much is it worth? In our saturated market democracies in which products have become more and more interchangeable, the last few years and decades have shown that there is one thing people want more than anything else: lower prices. The price has become the simplest and most reliable criterion with which we can differentiate between products. Cheap is becoming synonymous with 'good'. The development of democracies from the USA to Spain and Germany or the countries of the new Europe provides overwhelming proof that a life in time of peace is a life that defines itself according to the values of consumer democracy.[3] Participation in society means participation in political processes and in consumer choices.

People want a material basis that affords them a minimum of prosperity and choice. The leading Western economies – for example the USA or Germany – are the countries where the price is the most dominant instrument and in which democracy and consumption are most radically linked. At the same time, the most democratic countries in the world – and the USA and Germany are certainly two of them – are also those where success is hardest to achieve.[4] We can provide many examples of how difficult it is for foreign companies to gain a footing in the

German market. The French have not been successful in Germany, and even Wal-Mart has had great difficulty in understanding it and expanding its operations profitably on the German market. And the United States is the most difficult country for Europeans – again, think of the field of trade here: Ahold, the stock market darling in Europe until the beginning of this century, stumbled and was brought down by the scandal mentioned earlier because it misjudged the mentality and toughness of the market. Or just look at the very modest progress made in the USA by such European giants as Auchan or Sainsbury's. Success seems to be achievable only in niches – for example in fashion, where luxury ranges with their high margins are attractive. But for the masses and for mass trading, the United States is a tough nut to crack.

We can summarize the most important aspects of consumer democracy as the three As:

- *Accessibility.* Access is easy and, above all, no longer defined via specific traditional criteria. Whenever, wherever I want something, I can get it.
- *Affordability.* I don't have to be a millionaire to play the game. I can afford it. Financial barriers are being lowered. If I want something, I can get it at an affordable price.
- *Amenity.* The product must be intriguing, interesting, amusing and enlightening. Even low-priced products must offer values that are important to me personally and thus become part of my personal product universe. This can be seen most clearly in the premium sector. At the lower end of the market, a differentiation has arisen in the Age of Cheap with 'cheap chic' – cheap, but tasteful – an up-and-coming trend, from cars (Hyundai) to gourmet food (Trader Joe's) to fashion (Zara, H&M), and a trend that is placing the more upmarket segments under pressure. And of course the quality is also good. Welcome to the world of cheap chic!

In our age of consumer democracy, people are slowly getting used to the new realities of increasingly globalized markets. Their motto is of political origin, a slightly modified form of the famous motto of the French Revolution: Liberty, equality, money. You have a choice, you have equal access, irrespective of traditions, and in the end it is your wallet, your cash resources, that tips the scales. He who pays the piper calls the tune. He who calls the tune pays the piper. Fraternity, the quality of brotherliness, which was always the most problematical of the famous trilogy, is replaced by money, by affordability. 'How much money have you got?' is the all-important question. Thus, our money orientation or price orientation is the highest expression of a fully developed democratic consumer society: Liberty, equality and money. And it also means growing independence of political constraints with increasing responsibility for the individual.[5]

The four stages of development in customer behaviour[6]

If we summarize the progress of consumer democracy over the last few decades in a simple pattern, we can see four stages:

- *Stage 1: 'You need it!' – economies of needs.* In the beginning, economies were economies of supply. How could the supply of basic goods be ensured in a democracy? It was in pursuit of this aim that in many countries, for example, consumer cooperatives were formed in the food sector. The better the basic supply is ensured, the more the demand will be created for 'better' goods, in other words goods for the satisfaction of personal wishes, and more exotic, individual, tailor-made products and services.
- *Stage 2: 'You want it!' – economies of wants.* Needs can be met, but personal wishes and desires are infinitely more varied.[7]

The transition from an economy of needs to an economy of wants is perhaps the decisive step that defines how we organize ourselves, how we communicate with each other and how we decide to live our lives. Today, businesses have to master the art of seducing the customer again and again. 'Modernity means the freedom of seduction,' says Turkish social scientist Nilüfer Göle. The essence of freedom in an economy of wants is the continuing creation of new and desirable products. A consumer democracy, of course, also depends essentially on this. Without this engine, a consumer democracy cannot achieve its full potential.

- *Stage 3: 'You deserve it!' – economies of access, reward and instant gratification.* The more innovation, abundance and prosperity become a matter of course, the more important access to the product becomes. That is probably the core insight of the age of information. It is like access to the world wide web: we are no longer prepared to wait; we are increasingly impatient. The number of barriers is falling. On the one hand, the number of channels via which I can make purchases has increased enormously over the last few years. On the other hand, the number of channels via which I can access information has also increased dramatically over the same period of time.

- *Stage 4: 'You can!' – economies of discount: you do it just because you can – at the lowest price.* Today, we are entering into a phase where customers are so knowledgeable that they know their way around value creation chains, ranges of goods and services etc. Thus, strictly speaking, there are now only B2B (Business to Business) customers and no more B2C (Business to Consumer) customers. We buy simply because we can. If you can buy it, then do so, and at the lowest possible price! This development, too, makes innovation more difficult. What today is an exclusive, expensive product with luxury status will be a mere commodity tomorrow, just another barter or consumer product. We compare everything with everything else, and the tendency is for everything to be accorded equal value! The well-informed customer knows the price of everything – but the value of nothing.[8]

So we can say that discount orientation, the search for value and the focus on price, political economy and money are part of a comprehensive modernization process changing the mentality of customers and citizens today, at the beginning of an accelerated process of globalization.

The panorama of cheap

Let us take a brief look at the various sectors and segments. This will give us an overview of the widely varying phenomena that characterize our Age of Cheap.

Cheap fashion – clothes are becoming cheaper

Without a doubt, it is the fashion sector in which this phenomenon has taken strongest hold. Compared with foodstuffs and all other non-food segments, fashion has seen the widest development. This is because, in the fashion industry, everything, from production to distribution, can be de-localized with relative ease. Fashion is the fastest-moving sector. In both the premium and the discount segments, we can find many examples that illustrate that everything connected with fashion has become completely democratized. Zara[9] and H&M are probably among the most important pacesetters in the trade. These two rapidly expanding chains are able to offer their trend-conscious clientele attractively priced fashion, and their range changes several times a year or even weekly in the best cases.

However, the others are learning quickly, for example in the hypermarket and supermarket sector with proprietary brands such as Asda/Wal-Mart's George, Tesco's Cherokee or Sainsbury's Jeff range in the lower price segments. To ensure that they are not caught napping by this development, the upmarket labels are rapidly differentiating and defining new segments for themselves. The Armani X/Change and Versace Jeans Couture lines are examples that show how labels whose luxury status once frightened off the average buyer are now having to woo a more price-conscious clientele in order to reinforce the emotional identity of their higher-priced products from below and anchor their products in the consumer consciousness.

The hard discounters have also long recognized the potential of low-price fashion. Aldi already makes a turnover of over one billion euros with clothing and is thus the seventh-largest textile retailer in Germany. Lidl is not far behind, and Plus is experimenting with selling Ralph Lauren at prices 50 per cent below the regular retail prices (or are the articles only clever fakes?)[10]

Cheap food – food is getting (even) cheaper

Food is *the* domain of the hard discounters, particularly the German ones. At present, Aldi and Lidl are a success story in every country in which they operate.[11] This phenomenon is most pronounced in Germany. Aldi and Lidl are both catching up with the market leaders, even in countries where they have been less prominent so far, with Lidl the more aggressive of the two.[12] In the USA, the so-called Dollar Stores are even gaining ground on Wal-Mart and are growing at a faster rate than the market leader itself.[13] Here, five of the leading chains, Family Dollar, Dollar General, Dollar Tree, Fred's and 99 Cents Only, gained 15.8 per cent in 2002 compared with 2001, and experts predict similar growth as far as 2007. Dollar Stores already have more than 12,500 outlets in the USA, and, typical of a good discount concept, they are successfully exploiting new customer segments. Today, they reach 52 per cent of US households, and the figure is growing.[14] Their popularity rests above all on their credibility. Their prices are so low that consumers have the impression that the store really is helping them save money. Above all, what the consumer gets at Dollar Stores is the feeling of at least minimal empowerment, because Dollar Stores offer a mix of consumer products that even the poorest can afford. And even more, the customer can choose between different low-price products. Nowadays most people feel increasingly at the mercy of the state, powerless and treated indiscriminately. And the much smaller area of Dollar Stores creates a more familiar atmosphere and inspires more confidence than the big boxes at Wal-Mart. Customers don't want integrated pharmacies or chemist's stores; they don't want credit cards or extravagant services. They know instinctively that all these things only cost money and that it is they who will pay for them in the end in the form of higher prices.

Yet the Dollar Stores may also have a negative sociological effect. If only the poor or the very poorest people buy there, this reinforces social segregation. The same phenomenon that can be seen in the upper levels of society, namely an increasing homogenization of social life within social groups – members of a social class will shop in the same places, invest their money in the same way, send their children to the same schools, live in the same areas and use the same channels – can be seen increasingly among the lower classes.[15]

Wal-Mart does see the Dollar Stores as serious competition. The fact that the store giant is now experimenting with its own version of hard discounting proves that. Under the name 'Hey Buck', Wal-Mart is attempting to find out how it can counter the rise of the highly concentrated low-cost operators with the help of shop-in-shop concepts. Kroger was the first large-scale supermarket in the USA to develop this concept systematically and integrate it as a store-corner concept. However, it was a Swiss company that first recognized the trend, the supermarket and hypermarket retailer Migros. It attained cult status in the second half of the 1990s with several dozen articles, above all with food and near-food products, with the introduction of the M-Budget line, a subdivision of its own proprietary brand with a clear discount profile. But, and this is typical of Swiss companies, trends were not followed up consistently, and this – successful – campaign remained more of a one-off phenomenon, though it is now copied by many of the big stores from Kroger to Wal-Mart.

Regional suppliers, too, can get in on the action. In Switzerland, Denner is growing very quickly, and Colruyt in Belgium has had an unbelievable success story.[16] The formats that can boast positive growth rates are those with a clearly defined product range, without too much confusing diversity and, above all of course, with a no-frills cost structure. The low-cost food stores are also in a better position with regard to their size and location. While the classic formats such as super- or hypermarkets are becoming too complex and time-consuming – on the whole, they have probably peaked in the ripe markets, which is shown by the difficulty they are experiencing in creating new concepts, especially for hypermarkets – the hard discounters enjoy continuing growth.[17]

Cheap computers – computers at the end of the computer age

Larry Ellison, the charismatic CEO of Oracle, estimates that the computer industry as a whole has reached maturity and is now under increasing pressure to provide cheaper products, as the Next Big Thing is going to come not from the IT sector but from the field of biotechnology. And so cheap computers with free Linux software and increased efficiency will continue to push prices and margins down. The IT sector will have to introduce more standardization and simplify its products and services radically if it does not want to lose the fight against time and against the premature erosion of its margins right now. And the customer will benefit from all this.[18] Where will they be making cuts? Predominantly in services and consultancy services, because these are areas of low transparency, areas that are hard to second-guess. Few firms nowadays can afford the luxury of leading the field in development when the implementation of IT processes offers no guaranteed productivity bonus.

Cheap home improvement, cheap consumer electronics – enjoy entertainment in your own home for next to nothing

Let us take another example: the whole sector of appliances, household devices and furniture. In spite of their relatively complex organizational structures, companies like Media Markt, Saturn, Best Buy, Home Depot or Ikea can continue to cut prices – or at least give the customer the impression that their products are cheap. It is no coincidence that the Saturn advertising campaign 'Cheap is GOOD!' has been one of the most successful in the last few years. The slogan reflects a mentality that accurately sums up the spirit of the age.

Nowadays, if Ikea Switzerland announces that it will be selling a sofa for 30 Swiss francs, people will be camping out overnight in front of the stores in the hope of snapping up one of these coveted bargains, which is surprising in a country like Switzerland where it is well known that customers pay a good margin.[19] An important factor seems to be that home improvement is becoming cheaper. As it is increasingly likely nowadays that people will not be staying in one place for long, it is all the more important to have furnishings that are flexible, and this is achieved by buying lower-priced articles. At Ikea, I get not only low-cost furniture but furniture that enables me to keep abreast of ever-changing trends without having to spend a small fortune. The head of Ikea Germany, Werner Weber, sums it up: 'We will be positioning our prices even lower.'[20]

And in every household today, entertainment systems are standard equipment. The development of consumer electronics provides an impressive example of how quickly innovations become low-price articles. Records and vinyl were followed by the CD. The video industry has long since peaked. Consumers now want DVD quality. Flat screens are fascinating. We are moving towards a convergence of media, and the integration of sound, image and film allows us to get home entertainment equipment at lower and lower prices.

Cheap mobility, cheap travel – movement in discount

The most impressive example is without doubt the emotional sector of travel. If there is one thing the prosperity-sated people of the Western world – and, following their example, the threshold countries – are not prepared to give up, it is the opportunity to travel. Freedom and the right to travel whenever you want and wherever you want seem to be inextricably linked. And when the travel sector and unlimited mobility become the pacemaker for 'cheap', we have hit the essence of freedom as we understand it today. Nothing is more socially acceptable than unlimited mobility at unbeatable prices.

The airlines have provided an unparalleled example of how strongly and above all how quickly discount-driven economic and social modernization can oust old traditions. Hardly any other sector has seen such a strong increase in price sensitivity over the last few years. Whereas the national carriers – for example Swissair in Switzerland – were once symbols of national pride and prestige and enjoyed a high degree of acceptance even among non-flyers, this attitude is rapidly fading in the face of current market conditions. Cheap flights are now seen almost as a basic human right.

This is an international phenomenon and one that transcends all social classes. Not only economy-class but even pampered business-class passengers are flocking to the low-price operators in droves. Wherever you travel within Europe today, whether between Berlin and Zurich, Hamburg and London or Frankfurt and Paris, more and more business-class seats are empty. We are witnessing a rapid change in business class in our society and on short-haul flights it has virtually disappeared. Airlines continue to think in terms of prestige, while for most business travellers time has long become the most important factor. Business travellers are prepared to settle for less comfort, but they want to save time, in other words they want flights that take off and land punctually, and in this respect many of the low-price airlines are now more reliable than the national carriers. Travellers are even willing to put up with a minimum of leg space as long as they know that the flight will take only 55 minutes and as long as they can check their e-mails and make a few phone calls in the airport lounge before take-off.

Big changes are also taking place in the area of long-haul flights. It is no coincidence that first class is quietly disappearing on more and more routes. At the same time, Lufthansa is refitting Boeing 747s or Airbus A319s for C-class-only flights on some long-haul routes to the USA with a carefully chosen number of 48 seats. This at least restores some sense of tribal identity.

And what about first class? While over the last few years the first-class cabin became more and more the refuge of a separate business-upgrade class and so was increasingly occupied by people trading in their bonus miles rather than those paying the normal rate for business class, the old elite have long since moved on and now take to the air in their private jets. Airlines continue to cut costs on scheduled flights, and customers, who have been pampered in recent years, are going to have to get used to it. While the national airlines are carrying out a general downgrading towards no-frills offers in order to compete with the discounters, those who can afford to disregard such considerations are no longer using scheduled airline flights and are instead taking to the air with their most important business associates on private flights.

Cheap flights are not a US or a European phenomenon but have become commonplace almost all over the globe: companies such as Jet Blue in the USA, Germanwings, Ryanair or easyJet in Europe, Virgin Blue in Australia, Air Asia in Malaysia[21] or Skymark in Japan are clear proof that prestige and national orientation are a thing of the past in the travel sector once a rival company offers the same quality at a much lower price – the Irish airline Ryanair boasts on its website that it is '446% cheaper than Lufthansa'.[22] All these airlines have followed the example set by the originator of the idea, Southwest, founded in 1971. Looking back, it only seems surprising that it took so long for this trend to take hold against the subsidized national carriers. But it also shows that prestige – and a similar development can be observed in often highly subsidized luxury hotels – can often tempt investors to put their money into schemes that will never yield a decent return.

Low-price airlines are pioneers in the field of business models and have perfected the art of yield management. Like Aldi or many of the Dollar Stores in the food sector, for example, they are able to attract completely new customer segments. Once prices have dropped to a certain level, flights become attractive even for those who would not normally travel by plane. And above all, the completely new destinations they fly to make tourism possible in areas that were off the beaten track before. Ryanair boss O'Leary and easyJet boss Stelios Haji-Ioannou are not exactly modest about it. 'We are redistributing the population of modern-day Europe,' says Stelios, referring to the fact that, thanks to the Age of Cheap, peripheral regions are being added to the mainstream routes in Europe – passengers from previously unheard-of Scandinavian towns such as Haugesund in Norway or from Ireland are now taking weekend trips to

Carcassonne, Bergamo or Jerez. Young Brits enjoy discount parties with discount trips to Barcelona, Ibiza or Dublin. And Stelios adds: 'I meet a lot of people on our flights that don't have to make the stark choice between the sun in the south and business in the north.'[23]

And let us not forget private travel! Automobility remains a cult in our civilization and staunchly refuses to be downgraded to a mere commodity. In the Age of Cheap, however, used cars are becoming more important. People are less prepared to pay the full price. In the United States, this has resulted in ruinous discounts being offered on US cars in a desperate attempt to get rid of the stockpiles caused by overproduction before it is too late. Good second-hand cars, which have almost the same utility value as new cars, are going to become more attractive in the coming years, as we will be able to reap the benefit of unbelievable discounts. A two- or three-year-old BMW or Lexus with 50,000 kilometres on the clock is still an almost perfect car that you can drive for another 10 years, and it costs only a fraction of the original price. A one-year-old VW Phaeton 6-litre V12 that costs only half the price of a new one and has 20,000 kilometres on the clock is a real bargain.

The market for well-cared-for used cars is likely to boom in future. And it is no coincidence that Korean manufacturers such as Hyundai or Kia – which are slowly shedding their image as merely cheap cars and becoming more aesthetically pleasing – have seen excellent growth rates on the tough European car markets in recent years. In 2003, Wal-Mart began to experiment with selling second-hand cars and, only three years after its launch, eBay's eBay Motors[24] is by far the largest used-car dealer in the USA. There is less and less social prestige to be gained by buying overpriced goods. Here, too, customers are learning that new methods of personal market observation give them a decisive advantage. If you do your research thoroughly beforehand and then negotiate skilfully, you can strike a very good bargain.

As in the case of the cheap airlines, the sales channel will be of considerable importance: new customers, above all first-time buyers, can be attracted via new channels. The example of eBay Motors shows that it is possible to sell cars via the internet. Younger customers are much more flexible than customers who have become accustomed to always buying their products via the same channel.

Finally, mobility is increasingly a question of the mobility of information: it has become much cheaper to make telephone calls. The rates for conventional telephone networks and other charges have fallen. The fact that computers are omnipresent – in our navigation systems, in our shoes, in our refrigerators, in our sunglasses – means that we are gradually becoming accustomed to having all the necessary data available on demand wherever we may be. The privileged status of voice communication as compared with communication in written form will probably remain largely unchanged in the years to come. We speak in person to those who matter to us. Everyone else will get either a computerized, written message or, more and more often, nothing at all.

The telecommunications sector remains one of the key industries of the future.

Cheap money, cheap risk management – money on the move

A world of cheap is also dependent on cheap money. It will be interesting to see to what degree consumer democracy will affect financial services. Today, no area of commerce is more chaotic, more complex or more driven by human emotions than the field of finance – which means that this field is, on the whole, far from being efficient.[25] As far as consumer democracy is concerned, the current situation in this field is far from ideal. The range of financial services is basically at the same stage of development as at the beginning of the industrial era. The sector lacks simple standardizations that give transparency for the customer, above all in the field of investments. 'We need to democratize finance and bring advantages enjoyed by the clients of Wall Street to the customers of Wal-Mart,' says Yale economist Robert J Shiller in his book on the new financial order.[26]

Today, the subject of money is omnipresent in everyday life. In the course of globalization, people's awareness of risks changes and money acquires more of a fetish character. The more uncertain the waters, the greater the hunger for guarantees, because only if you have money can you hoard for the future. It's always good to have money.

It seems only logical that this will also change the way we see money. The moral barriers that made us shy away from seeking our own financial advantage or running up debts are falling. The trend towards the latter is alarmingly prevalent among young people. Growing up in a world of abundance in which everything they could possibly want is available, for them money also acquires the status of permanent availability. 'Get it while you can!' seems to be the motto. In Europe, we have not yet reached the same level of consumer debt as in the United States, but mentally we are moving in the same direction.

Dramatic developments during the dot.com euphoria also provide evidence of a similar trend. The collateral damage is ongoing. 'Enrichissez-vous' becomes a legitimate motto, and the bosses in the world of big business continue to show us how it's done.[27] The more insecure our managers' jobs are, the more financial compensation managers receive – automatically and before they lift a finger. The higher the chances that I will lose my job immediately if I do not meet certain targets, the greater my desire for financial security. Rewards are paid for services not yet rendered and risks not yet taken. Performance and the financial reward for that performance are no longer firmly linked. Where we make comparisons nowadays, we compare monetary values.[28] And so it is no coincidence that providers of financial services are slowly but surely beginning to lose their supposedly unassailable social status.

Put it like this: the only reward that counts in a democratic market economy is money. There is no other yardstick. In a religious culture, the yardstick is piety. In a warrior culture, the way to earn honour is through bravery. In our society, you get money. This seems a tautology: because money is increasingly important, money becomes increasingly important. Honour is risible and has become at most an empty ritual. Piety only enters into the scheme of things in moments of existential crisis. Only money remains, because money promises the freedom to hoard for the future and to reduce one's dependence on uncertain private or state institutions. And thus money becomes even more of a game and a cult.

It is no coincidence that gambling has become so much more popular. And the change in the importance of Wall Street over the past five years speaks volumes.[29] The age-old sense of awe and tradition has disappeared as if it had never been. No one feels respect for the Wall Street banker any more. When it became known, after an endless series of financial scandals, that the chairman and CEO of the New York Stock Exchange himself, Richard A Grasso, had awarded himself US $139 million in compensation on top of his normal annual salary of US $10 million, all belief in the existence of moral integrity on Wall Street was lost. Ego tactics and personal gambles have become rife. And above all, in an online world, everyone gets to hear of it.

Because money is no longer linked to clearly defined and verifiable services rendered, people lose faith in institutions. If it is no longer clear for what someone is being paid or what you are paying a particular price for, the concept of fate automatically begins to reappear. So we have a sober, modern world in which – paradoxically – behaviour can only be explained in religious terms. Everything simply becomes a matter of fate. One person is lucky and is in the right place at the right time, while another has the simple misfortune to be in the wrong place at the wrong time. Yet for sensible people whom the state and other supportive organizations have always helped so far, this is hard to accept. And the consequence is that our faith in the system is replaced by faith in money. In a time of increasing insecurity in all areas, our faith in the system dips towards zero. We no longer trust the system, the state, the bank or any other hitherto legitimated institution. We only trust money, which we either have or do not have.

Thus money is a way of keeping options open for the future, and money itself ensures trust. So, where money is concerned, we can say without further ado that we are already living in a demoralized world. Now let us summarize this change in the significance of money and apply our insights to the subject of cheap money:

- *In the Age of Cheap, money is everything.* What counts is cash resources. What counts for products and services is, logically, the price. When we compare, we compare prices. Anything that is not monetary is monetarized. This boosts the power of the financial markets over the real markets again.[30] Anyone who fails to understand the mechanisms of the financial markets will also be unable to understand the mechanisms of the real markets.

- *In the Age of Cheap, gambling is freed from the taint of evil.* Playing for money is rapidly becoming the most important leisure activity in the developed nations. Whereas playing for money was formerly frowned upon in our cultural circles – especially in Germany – and expressions like casino capitalism or speculation were polemical terms that formed part of the vocabulary of dyed-in-the-wool socialists, with the accelerated change in society we are now seeing a fundamental change in the way casinos are seen. In the USA,[31] gambling already accounts for 8 per cent of

GNP compared with the mere 6 per cent contribution of family grocery. There has been a dramatic increase in spending money on legal gambling alone. Whereas Americans spent a mere US $17.3 billion on gambling in 1976, that figure had risen to US $586.5 billion by 1996 and it is estimated to be in the region of US $1 trillion at the time of writing. In particular, there has been a boom in so-called 'commercial gambling' as compared with leisure gambling activities, so that we can say that a process of fusion is taking place. Casinos, horse racing, sports bets, charity bingo, TV games, cyber-auctions – even the stock market – are all melting together to form one vast gambling network.[32] Today, gambling is the most popular form of entertainment in Japan and the USA, and the internet is accelerating this development.

- *In the Age of Cheap, it is particularly important that risk manage-ment should be brought down to the level of the Wal-Mart customer* (Shiller's plea). Only when people are in a position to evaluate and understand their financial position are they in a position to make informed decisions on how to invest and plan for the future. Politically, it will be of crucial importance whether or not we succeed in instilling in people a confidence in their ability to assume responsibility for their own fate while at the same time providing an institutional link-up. So above all, the Age of Cheap means that access to investments and the explanation of risk standards need to be radically simplified.

Cheap know-how, cheap consulting – knowledge as a cheap commodity

First, let us define knowledge as a form of know-how that is not highly specialized and can be written down, passed on and applied in the form of prescriptions, such as, for example, typical management know-how as best practice. This type of knowledge becomes a more and more easily exchanged commodity in a networked world. Kjell Nordstrøm calls this type of knowledge 'articulated knowledge' as compared to 'tacit' or passive knowledge. Articulated knowledge is knowledge that has to be efficient and effective and stir the masses. Tacit knowledge is either traditional knowledge such as manual skills handed down over generations, which it is difficult to copy, or can take the form of highly specialized, abstract scientific research knowledge that is (still) far from ready for commercial exploitation.

The business schools are the best example of how mass application knowledge has changed dramatically in the last few years. Twenty years ago, perhaps even 10 years ago, various theories were taught. Nowadays, in our connected world, it does not take long before all lecturers know and are teaching exactly the same thing. If you take an MBA course, you don't hear anything new about marketing. You are taught the 45th edition of Philip Kotler's views on marketing management. And if you want to learn something about strategic positioning, they dish up the 53rd edition of Michael Porter. This means that, in a connected world, the tendency is for everyone to have the same knowledge and to express the same opinions. The head start that knowledge once gave us is shrinking.[33]

The same is true of consultants, who often copy or reinterpret the concepts and case studies drawn up by the business schools to suit their own requirements. And as there is a surplus of consultants, there will be a boom in discount consulting. Knowledge can be bought in multipacks! In short, knowledge is becoming cheaper, loses its value increasingly and is thus less and less likely to provide that competitive edge. The value of an MBA is decreasing, even though the title itself may still seem desirable.[34] We have made no progress in our efforts to use knowledge as an instrument of differentiation.

Cheap beauty – body design according to the McBody rule

One of the fastest-growing global markets is the whole beauty sector. The beauty industry is estimated to have had a total volume of US $160 billion in 2003. The more people are forced to concentrate on core values in order to survive in everyday life, the more important anthropological constants become and the more emphasis is placed on them in the mass markets – attractiveness, approval, sex. Skin care (US $24 billion), make-up products (US $18 billion), hair care products (US $38 billion) and perfumes (US $15 billion) are growing at a rate of 7 per cent per annum. And here, too, discounting is increasingly important. This trend even extends far beyond the area of skin care and personal hygiene alone, to reconstructional medicine and cosmetic surgery. Whereas 10 years ago the reconstruction of one female breast cost US $10,000, according to leading US plastic surgeon Alan Matarasso it is now possible for a mere US $600. And the people who pay to have such operations performed are no longer the rich. Seventy per cent of patients come from the lower middle class and have an annual income of less than US $50,000.[35] The pressure to 'look and feel good' has increased enormously.

In the USA today, people are already spending more money on 'looking and feeling good' every day than on education or further training. Cosmetic surgery is a market with a volume of US $20 billion, and one that has seen an increase of 220 per cent since 1997. And that is without including the whole sector of well-being, which is difficult to pinpoint, as there is a lot of convergence in this area. The globalization of information has created new standards for beauty – global beauty. Traditional or national ideas of beauty are quickly cast aside in favour of individual choices.[36] China or South Korea provides examples of how cheap beauty has become a mass market that puts its money on 'cheap'. Plastic surgeons, frequently unqualified, offer almost any service under the sun for less than US $100. From skin treatment to simple or more complex operations, injections such as those with botox or tooth whitening, there's hardly anything you can't get there.

An impressive example of how to define a new discount market is provided by Kuniyoshi Konishi in Japan. Japan is a country where customers tend to follow traditional rituals in order not to stand out from the crowd. Having a standard haircut takes one hour and can cost between 3,000 and 6,000 yen (approximately 23 to 46 euros). Konishi found this ritual ridiculous, time-consuming and inappropriate and began to wonder whether it would not be possible to get the job done in only 10 minutes and for 1,000 yen. It *is* possible, and today Mr Konishi has over 200 hairdressing salons that have achieved the seemingly impossible under the name QBNet.

How this discount system is organized to make it profitable is a wonderful story. To get as quick a turnaround as possible, it was necessary to strip away all activities that have nothing to do with the core competence of 'cutting hair'. Instead of a till with change or credit cards there is a machine into which you insert a 1,000-yen note, thus avoiding the need for change. The machine dispenses a ticket, which customers give to the hairdresser before taking their place on the chair. The salons have no telephone, so you can't make an appointment – that would only hold things up. Instead of the stylist washing and drying your hair, this is done by a wash-and-dry system suspended from the ceiling, and when your hair is cut the ends are sucked off through a hose. So that customers can see whether they will have to wait or not, there are sensors attached to each chair, and a display at the entrance to the salon shows people outside whether they can get their hair cut straight away (green light), whether there is a five-minute wait (amber light) or whether the wait will be longer (red light). Each salon chair is also automatically linked via internet to the group's headquarters in Tokyo. As on the airlines, turnover can be calculated in real time. If business booms in a particular location, a further salon will be opened there as soon as possible.[37] This example also illustrates that it is possible to be successful on highly regulated markets that are extremely conventional as far as customer behaviour is concerned. It's not a question of breaking the rules; you just have to make them flexible, says the president of QBNet, Koji Araki.

Cheap porn, cheap death, cheap morals – the cheapening of intimacy

That the phenomenon of cheap is not simply an ephemeral one that applies to standard consumer goods, but instead one that has permeated all levels of social activity, is easy to prove. Even sectors of business activity that have always been conducted locally and in an intimate and discreet atmosphere, such as for example pornography or death, are now a familiar sight in the media and are affected by developments in the Age of Cheap. Cheap porn – the globalization of the pornography industry – brings with it standardization and price pressure.[38] Here, too, modern technology – in this case, the internet – has accelerated the development. Western European producers of porn videos and internet porn sites employ actors and actresses from Eastern Europe for the simple reason that they work faster and do more for less. And so Budapest has become a more important production location than Amsterdam or Copenhagen.[39]

Or take the extreme case of cheap death. With globalization and the increased pressure to keep costs low, death, too, becomes something you can get at a discount.[40] The largest company, SCI Services Corporation International in Houston, owns several thousand so-called funeral service locations, with hundreds of cemeteries and crematoria in 20 countries and on all five continents. Their main product is death services, everything connected with death. They offer people a comprehensive package of every service they might require at the painful time of bereavement. The main markets are France, Canada and the USA for the full service, but also several Latin American countries, Australia and Great Britain.

What we are experiencing here is nothing less than a wide-reaching flexibilization of our moral concepts. We are becoming even more pragmatic, or hyperpragmatic. Not only do we adjust our opinions and our reasoning immediately to suit the moment, but we also adjust our moral concepts to real time, so to speak.[41] And so morals, too, are becoming cheaper.[42]

Developments in the areas of products and services also have their effect on a symbolic level. People do not change the way they behave in a revolutionary, but rather in an evolutionary, manner. That explains why we ourselves hardly notice how we are changing. The message to the customer in the Age of Cheap is: demand more for less. What today's customers expect first and foremost is low prices. Low prices are the fuel driving the bulldozer of globalization. There is no power more direct, more emotionally effective than the seduction offered by even lower prices. And there is nothing more democratic than easy access and free choice for all. Shopping may be a burden, but there is no better alternative. The only alternative to shopping is better shopping. And in a market democracy where access is facilitated, this will always mean: even faster, better, cheaper.

The manufacturers of Colgate toothpaste spent a fortune on training us to believe that, if we used this brand of toothpaste every day, we would have white teeth all our lives. It worked. We still believe today that we can increase the life expectancy of our teeth and retain their whiteness by cleaning them thoroughly every day. But what if they now tell us that, thanks to the latest technology, we no longer need toothpaste at all and that we can have perfect teeth immediately and much more cheaply? If we can have 'instant white' at the drop of a hat and at a low price, then that is much better than having to scrub your teeth laboriously every day for decades! What if they teach us that we can 'feel and look good' at the press of a button and for less and less money? That means not only are we getting cheap beauty and adjusting our ideals of beauty to suit the requirements of the age but our morals, too, are of the here-and-now and price conscious. Cheap morals become more and more important. In a complex and dynamic economic world, morals, too, are flexible and our behaviour much more pragmatic. As customers, we increasingly follow the 'works/doesn't work' principle. If it works, it's OK; if it doesn't work, then it doesn't and is therefore bad.

Cheap cities – the downgrading of our inner cities

Our urban centres are also changing. In rural areas, the range of services available to the consumer underwent a change many years ago. The village baker, the butcher, the shoe shop and the clothes shop disappeared from village life for reasons of cost or due to lack of demand. It has proved possible to ensure supplies to the rural population – at the time, concerns were voiced as to whether this could be done. Shopping centres have sprung up on what were once green fields, supplying mainly foodstuffs, and we get to them by car. Now, an analogous process is taking place, a few years later but at an alarming pace, in our inner cities. Many well-established and mostly local suppliers can no longer afford to pay the high rents charged for premium locations. They are being replaced by large national or more frequently international chains with a cheaper image: many of the big chains such as Starbucks, Zara or Grand Optical deliberately seek out these central locations as it is only here that they can ensure a quick turnaround and profits. Simultaneously, non-food hypermarkets have been springing up in the green belts: Ikea, Media Markt, Toys 'R' Us, Decathlon, Obi etc. The next development will be a Europe-wide increase in the number of amusement parks. We can already predict that competition will become even keener. And more than ever, whether you are competitive or not is in the end a question of price.

Nowadays, when we hear the names of many large European cities, we think, among other things, of their famous shopping miles and exclusive shopping areas. However, this is already changing. On the one hand, many new shopping facilities are being created as stations, museums and old industrial buildings are converted into shopping centres. Over-banking, or the over-presence of banking services, has already left its mark. Many branches have been streamlined or closed down, and many more will follow. Such premises are often converted to shops. The too great variety of shops in premium shopping locations where high rents are charged eats into the profits of the well-established businesses that cannot be subsidized out of the coffers of international group headquarters.

The result is increasingly homogeneous shopping in urban centres. Visit Düsseldorf or Zurich or Munich or Barcelona, and you will see more and more of the same chain stores. They are smart, have an attractive range of goods to offer and, above all, their prices are competitive. Actually, that's wonderful, you might think. But what soon becomes obvious is a certain monotony of style. The range can quickly seem trivial, and the excitement factor and the goods that were specific to that particular location have gone, cut in order to ensure that the price stays low. Zurich provides a very good example of this process in action. The once famous Bahnhofstrasse is gradually becoming 'cheaper'. Old-established businesses such as Séquin Dormann are leaving and in their place you have Mango, Grand Optical, Fielmann, The Body Shop, H&M or WE, plus a good selection of discount perfumeries. Fnac[43] is opening a large store there. The interesting thing about this development is that the phenomenon of cheap is invading even our old-established urban centres of luxury shopping, and it is here to stay. And in step with this development, the surrounding area will also change: it, too, will become 'cheaper'.

Cheap chic – cheap brands? Cheap doesn't mean lousy!

Of course, in some cultures, the word 'cheap' has a nasty taste to it. But let us be perfectly clear here: cheap doesn't have to have negative connotations and be synonymous with lousy! The days have long gone when the average consumer – for example in that bastion of high prices, Switzerland – was convinced that an article that is 10 times more expensive must therefore be 10 times better. A product that costs 10 euros is not necessarily five times better than a product that costs 2 euros. A closer look at the panorama of cheap clearly confirms this: the prestige that was once associated with being able to afford to pay high prices is not as high as it was. We are becoming more prosaic and slowly realizing that, just because something is cheap, it does not have to mean it's bad.

In glutted markets, cheap – see, for example, Aldi or Wal-Mart – means a combination of factors, namely inexpensive, good quality and simplicity. Companies that are able to offer the consumer excellent prices and at the same time good and increasingly good quality will be successful. So the trend towards cheap products does not have to be seen as entirely negative. The fact that Aldi and Lidl are so successful has a lot to do with simplicity and their ability to provide good orientation. The hard discounters have the additional advantage of being within easy reach. As the sales area of their stores is relatively small, the chances are good that you will find one within a convenient distance of your home. In this way, they help the customer to save personal resources – for example time, the stress factor, the hunt for information. These, too, are success factors typical of the modernization of our society that is taking place parallel to that of our economies.

Cheap is going to change our markets from the bottom up. There is also the factor of differentiation. When everything is getting cheaper, when the focus is on the price, you carve out a niche for yourself by being cheap but tasteful. Cheap chic has a great future. As we have already mentioned, Plus is selling Ralph Lauren fashion at 50 per cent lower prices! And H&M or Zara usually has trendily dressed sales personnel, too. You can get hardware by industrial designers at Target (the Americans pronounce it almost lovingly in the French way, as 'Tarzhay'). The big difference between Target and Wal-Mart is that Target is a company that immediately picks up on and reacts to retail trends, whereas Wal-Mart's pace is determined by its IT system. And, of course, there is cheap chic in the airline sector with Jet Blue. The cabin crew wear suits by Prada, and on Jet Blue flights you are served delicious biscotti, not the usual inedible salted peanuts dripping with fat.

The most intriguing company offering cheap chic in the food sector has to be Trader Joe's. The aim of this chain, which is based in Monrovia, Los Angeles, is much less ideological than that of Aldi[44] or Wal-Mart – it aims to offer the customer an inexpensive range of gourmet food in establishments of a size that makes sense. Trader Joe's buys directly from the producers, guided by the criterion of taste and quality – and is on average 20 per cent cheaper than the other suppliers of gourmet foods. Eighty per cent of the goods are sold under a private label, though the company takes a very pragmatic attitude to this subject. They are not dependent on the big food producers. If they can get organic foods at a reasonable price, then they will sell organic foods. And if it's healthy into the bargain, all the better. Trader Joe's is growing fast with around 200 stores (mainly on the East and West Coast) with an average area of a little more than 1,000 square metres and a turnover of approximately $2 billion.

If you study trading chains and how customer-oriented they are, you could become quite a fan of Trader Joe's. There are few stores where you will feel such a positive energy. The staff are generally also highly motivated and support the customer in a very pleasing manner. They provide accurate and brief information as required and do not get on your nerves by being ignorant or know-it-all. The interior decor of the stores is simple but tasteful and shows much attention to detail. In contrast to the equally successful organic food chain Whole Foods, which targets a wealthier clientele, as the store fittings, the packaging and the prices show, at Trader Joe's the impression is that here reason, ambience and price orientation have reached an almost perfect synthesis.

Another fantastic example of cheap chic is the magazine *Budget Living*,[45] launched in October 2002. The name itself, combining budget and living or lifestyle, sums up what the magazine is all about. It is also a perfect expression of the zeitgeist, offering the reader tips on achieving a certain lifestyle – differentiation via taste – but at low prices. It shows me, for example, how I can invite 10 friends around and conjure up a five-course dinner with only one hour's preparation, including shopping and cooking, serving a meal that costs only a modest amount per guest and still includes champagne, Italian mineral water, Asian cuisine and a dessert buffet.

The cheap chic trend is hardly imaginable without the trend towards proprietary brands. This means that the branded goods, even the most upmarket of them, are going to come under increasing pressure. As far as I know, there is no study that indicates that brand loyalty increases with increasing choice, better-informed consumers, greater price pressure and more price orientation. In other words, the cheap brands will also play a significant role in future, and private labels or proprietary brands/retailer's own brands will continue to gain ground on the established brands.[46] For some years now, this has been a global trend – a phenomenon seen not only in Europe or North America, but increasingly also in Asia, Latin America and the emerging markets. This in turn forces manufacturers to find new strategies in their dealings with customers. Skilful marketing campaigns for your brand are no longer enough. It goes without saying that branded goods will still be relevant, but there are more and more alternatives, and this leads to a weaker bond with the customer, because if I am disappointed I can switch to another brand immediately without losing money. The lower the switching costs, the more endangered a brand is.[47]

In summary, we can say that the same applies to the development taking place in private life, in shopping and consumer behaviour as to that taking place in our democracies or in political life. It is not the best possible form of government, but the least unpleasant: 'Consumerism is not pretty, but it beats the alternatives put forward so far.'[48] Political dictatorships are going to come under increasing pressure in a networked world where there is easy access to information. The force of galloping globalization inevitably brings with it the desire for prosperity and personal happiness – and once this desire has been awakened, it seems to be stronger than our love of or loyalty to political systems. The bulldozer rolls on, with all the contradictions it creates. In connection with the bulldozer of globalization, we can also see a further analogy between political and economic developments: there is an axis of evil in economic life, too. However, depending on our standpoint, we could also call it the axis of good.

The elements of this axis are interconnected and, without them, the bulldozer would not be so important.

Notes

[1] This is the conclusion of an interview I conducted with Nathan Gardels, editor of *News Perspective Quarterly* (*NPQ*), at the beginning of August 2003 in Los Angeles.

[2] These are also questions asked by Kjell Nordstrøm and Jonas Ridderstrale in their new book *Karaoke Capitalism*, published in 2004.

[3] We saw this when East and West Germany were reunited. The first thing East Germans wanted was the West German Mark and then – more concretely – bananas.

4   See the discount study carried out by the Institute for Grocery Distribution, 'Future focus – European discount retailing', published 20 December 2002. It describes in detail the development towards discounting.

5   It is probably inevitable that this means that social considerations and the family play a minor and dependent role. Mechanisms to compensate for this will be developed. On the subject of the future of the family and the new role of woman, see the GDI studies 'The future of woman' and 'The future of the family' (2003) by Karin Frick and Lars Feldmann respectively, GDI studies Nos. 7 and 8.

6   For more recent theories on consumer behaviour, see Thomas Hine (2002) *I Want That! How we all became shoppers*, Harper Collins, New York; Daniel Miller (1998) *A Theory of Shopping*, Polity, New York; and, impressive as always, the books of James B Twitchell, eg *Lead Us into Temptation: The triumph of American materialism*, Columbia University Press, New York, 1999, and, historically interesting, Gary Cross (2000) *An All-Consuming Century: Why commercialism won in modern America*, Columbia University Press, New York. These books all work from the premise that shopping is inevitably attractive: the alternative to shopping is better shopping. The opposite view is held by the often-quoted works of Juliet Schor, Arlie Russell Hochschild and Barbara Ehrenreich.

7   See Norbert Bolz and David Bosshart (1995) *Kult-Marketing: Die neuen Götter des Marktes*, Econ, Düsseldorf.

8   To describe the situation by paraphrasing Oscar Wilde.

9   José Luis Nueno from the University of Navarro in Barcelona has studied Zara in depth. His findings are discussed in detail in a GDI study entitled 'The Age of Cheap' (2004), which he co-authored.

10 See 'Designermode auf dem Grabbeltisch', *Der Spiegel*, No. 42/2003, p 88.

11 See the above-mentioned GDI study on the European discount trade.

12 See George MacDonald, 'From a Lidl to a lot', *Retail Week*, 10 October 2003, p 20.

13 The importance of foodstuffs in the range varies from one Dollar Store to another.

14 Much of my information on the Dollar Stores was supplied by Candace Corlett, a partner in WSL Strategic Retail in New York. On the subject of the development of the low-cost operators, see *DSN Retailing Today*, **42** (14), 21 July 2003, pp 1, 26; also Francis Lecompte, 'L'irrésistible percée des néo-discounters américains', *LSA*, No. 1832, 16 October 2003, pp 22–24.

15 This is one of the central themes in Robert B Reich's (2001) book *The Future of Success*, Alfred A Knopf, New York. See in particular the chapter 'The community as commodity', pp 194–213.

[16] See Dan Bilefsky, 'Making the cuts', *Wall Street Journal Europe*, 26–28 September 2003, pp R2, R7.

[17] This is true, for example, of the home of the hypermarkets, France, where hypermarket market shares fell between 2000 and 2003 (from 53.6 per cent to 51.8 per cent) and supermarkets fell from 36 per cent to 35 per cent, while the hard discounters (the four largest, namely Aldi, Ed, Leader Price and Lidl) went from 9 per cent to 11 per cent in the same period – information taken from the leading French trade journal *LSA*, No. 1830, 2 October 2003, p 23.

[18] See Mylene Mangalindan, 'Larry Ellison's sober vision: Tech industry will shrink, 1000 companies will fail, predicts Oracle's feisty chief', *Wall Street Journal*, 8 April 2003, p B1.

[19] It is no coincidence that such phenomena are being observed in Switzerland, but it is a source of annoyance to other customers – namely to those who turn up at the store at opening time, only to discover that they are too late. See 'Eine Nacht im Freien für ein 30-Franken-Sofa: Kritik an Ikea-Aktion', *Neue Zürcher Zeitung*, No. 206, 6/7 September 2003, p 59.

[20] See 'Möbelkonzern Ikea will billiger werden', *Handelsblatt*, No. 220, 14–16 November 2003, p 16. Ikea's main aim here is to compete against furniture discounters such as Poco, Boss or Roller and to expand its own customer segments. Some prices are to be cut by up to 30 per cent.

[21] See Trish Saywell and Scott Neuman, 'Budget air carriers are flying high in Asia', *Wall Street Journal Europe*, 3 July 2003, p A9.

[22] The question is how far – and for how long – politicians will intervene here to support and protect the national carriers for reasons of prestige. See also '"Asian Branson" charts a steady ascent', *Financial Times*, 14 October 2003, p 13.

[23] Quotation taken from *Wired*, March 2002.

[24] See www.ebaymotors.com.

[25] This is also the reason for the change in mood among leading economists in the last few years. The representatives of the so-called efficient market hypothesis, the most prominent of them at the University of Chicago, have dominated the discussion during the past decades. Today, more credence is given to the behavioural finance theories, which paint a more differentiated picture of human activity and produce answers more in keeping with the complexity of the situation. See Andrei Schleifer (2000) *Inefficient Markets: An introduction to behavioral finance*, Oxford University Press, New York; Robert J Shiller (2000) *Irrational Exuberance*, Princeton University Press, Princeton, NJ; or the many wonderful examples in Richard H Thaler (1992) *The Winner's Curse: Paradoxes and anomalies of economic life*, Princeton University Press, Princeton, NJ. It is probably also no coincidence that a representative of the behavioural finance theories, Daniel Kahneman, was awarded the Nobel Prize for Economics in 2002.

[26] Robert J Shiller (2003) *The New Financial Order: Risk in the 21st century*, Princeton University Press, Princeton, NJ, p 1.

[27] See Stephen M Pollan and Mark Levine (2000) *Enrichissez-vous! Le travail ne fais pas le bonheur, l'argent si*, Le cherche midi, Paris.

[28] When you ask European top managers to justify their rising salaries and the fact that they are not performance-linked, you will always receive the same answer: 'My colleagues in the USA earn a lot more!'

[29] See, for example, Howard Kurtz (2000) *The Fortune Tellers: Inside Wall Street's game of money, media and manipulation*, Free Press, New York. The book deals with all the most important topics, but reading it you get the irresistible impression that today Wall Street is more part of the entertainment business than a serious financial centre. See also Doug Henwood (1997) *Wall Street: How it works and for whom*, Verso, New York. Henwood's book paints an even gloomier picture, as it tries to shed light on the power mechanisms. Henwood's core statement is particularly depressing: Wall Street has as much power as the government itself, but its financial market activities contribute nothing to the real markets or to creating jobs. And if, as I maintain in this book, the real markets are starting to mimic the financial markets, we also have to ask ourselves whether the real markets will not then also adopt the management structures of the financial markets – and that would really be bad news.

[30] See the section 'Real Markets mimic financial markets' in Chapter 5.

[31] See Timothy L O'Brien (1998) *Bad Bet: The inside story of the glamour, glitz and danger of America's gambling industry*, Random House, New York.

[32] See source cited above.

[33] This, of course, does not mean that titles are worthless, but simply that the business schools can no longer claim to hold exclusive knowledge. The consequence is that the business schools set more and more store by their brand and the renown of their professors. Competence is no longer able to survive without prominence. And still the value sinks.

[34] It is no coincidence that, in the last few years, several thousand MBA courses, titles etc have appeared on the market. They all say more or less the same, and so the common jocular interpretation of MBA as 'mediocre but arrogant' is not so far off the mark.

[35] Goldman Sachs/*The Economist*, 24 May 2003.

[36] See Fred Guterl and Michael Hastings, 'The global makeover', *Newsweek*, 10 November 2003, pp 50–55.

[37] See Jim Hawe, 'A new style: QBNet had an idea – fast, cheap haircuts', *Wall Street Journal Europe*, 26–28 September 2003, p R2, or the many websites on which thousands vent their frustration with the discounters.

[38] See the chapter 'Sex, death and the welfare state' in John Micklethwait and Adrian Wooldridge (2000) *A Future Perfect: The challenge and hidden promise of globalisation*, Crown Business, New York, pp 78–96.

[39] For a comprehensive overview, see Dennis Altman (2001) *Global Sex*, University of Chicago Press, Chicago, IL; also Laurence O'Toole (1998) *Pornocopia: Porn, sex, technology and desire*, Serpent's Tail, London.

[40] See source cited above, pp 84f.

[41] Richard Sennett describes this very well in *The Corrosion of Character*, Norton, New York, 1998. This kind of softening of our moral concepts brings with it a corruptibility of our attitudes. Our moral concepts are literally corroded or eaten away. The central point is the corruptibility that is inevitable given present conditions.

[42] On the subject of the commercialization of human emotion, see in particular the classic works by Arlie Russell Hochschild: *The Commercialization of Intimate Life: Notes from home and work*, University of California Press, Berkeley, CA, 2003, and *The Managed Heart: Commercialization of human feeling*, University of California Press, Berkeley, CA, 1983 and 2003.

[43] The French Fnac chain is part of PPR Pinault-Printemps-Redoute, a group operating in the more downmarket, cheaper sector with channels such as Conforama and Fnac, but whose strategy is to offer a luxury line with, for example, Gucci and Yves Saint Laurent parallel to this. This combination is, of course, typical of the overall development in commerce: on the one hand, a concentration on more discounted articles and lower prices and, on the other hand, more differentiation in the luxury segment.

[44] This is even although, in 1979, the Albrecht brothers (owners of Aldi) were astute enough to buy the Trader Joe's chain, which was established in 1958.

[45] The magazine was launched in October 2002 and was an immediate success.

[46] Many studies on this subject have already been conducted at universities and above all by firms of consultants. For this reason, it will suffice to mention just one of the more recent studies, that by AC Nielsen Global Services (2003), *The Power of Private Label*. The consequence is dramatic but clear: the relationship between retailers and manufacturers will become even more critical.

[47] Markets that have not already gone through the four steps of development in consumerism mentioned above are – for the present, at least – safe ground for the big brands, above all the growth markets in Asia. Travelling within Europe, I find the same hotel chains in all the big cities. In Asia this is not the case, so that, as a result of the more limited choice, there is a greater chance that I will choose a Mandarin Oriental in Kuala Lumpur or Jakarta or the Grand Hyatt in Shanghai.

[48] James B Twitchell (2000) 'The Stone Age', in *Do Americans Shop Too Much?*, ed Juliet Schor, Beacon Press, Boston, MA, pp 44–48, 47.

2 The axis of evil in the economy

Wal-Mart, China and the internet

President George W Bush coined the term 'axis of evil', using it for the first time on 29 January 2002. He used it to describe the axis of nations or political unions that could, as a result of their disposition of power, threaten world peace. If we look a little more closely, we will see that we can also identify such an axis in the business world, an axis that could threaten 'world peace'. And every individual can choose whether to call this axis an 'axis of evil' or an 'axis of good'.

The first axis: trade – Wal-Mart and the message, 'Demand more for less!'

No one embodies the bulldozer as perfectly as Wal-Mart. Today, Wal-Mart is the largest retailer and the largest company in the world, with a gigantic stock market capital and amazing growth figures that have been in the two-digit range practically ever since the founding of the company in 1963. In 2003, its turnover exceeded US $250 billion. Wherever Wal-Mart appears on the scene, it is the benchmark for everyone else. Nowadays, Wal-Mart is practically unrivalled. It is bigger than all the other famous US trading giants such as Sears, Target, Kmart, JC Penny, Safeway and Kroger put together and generates more cash flow than all of them together. Every week, more than 138 million customers visit a Wal-Mart store. On one peak day, Wal-Mart opened 47 new stores – amazing when you think that they usually have a surface area of over 10,000 square metres! US economists believe that the company has played a significant role in keeping the inflation rate so low. According to McKinsey, Wal-Mart accounted for 12 per cent of the productivity gains in the United States in the second half of the 1990s.

Wal-Mart is the biggest customer of some of the world's most important companies – for example Walt Disney or Procter & Gamble. Because it buys its goods direct, various nations have direct access to the company's pipeline. Potential suppliers immediately become part of the Wal-Mart digital system. Wal-Mart tends to dictate everything from the price to the packaging. Wal-Mart employs about 1.4 million people. Wherever Wal-Mart appears on the scene with its trading concepts in the USA today, its competitors are likely to give up without a fight – often voluntarily and as quickly as possible. It is Wal-Mart's declared aim to offer low-priced goods – this at least is the message that comes across to the customer. The company wants to lower its customers' cost of living. Continually. The all-important question for us is: why do they do it? And the answer is as simple as it is surprising: because they can. Wal-Mart cuts prices simply because the company is in a position to do so, because it has tremendous purchasing power and keeps its costs low. In the USA, Wal-Mart is the market leader in almost every retail-relevant product group. In its channels Discount, Supercenter, Sam's Club and Neighborhood Store, and now with its new Grocery Supercenters, it leads the field in cat food, diamonds, car tyres, wine, toys, furniture and foodstuffs.

And by the way, Wal-Mart can exercise its symbolic power everywhere without having to be present in every country for it to do so. Wal-Mart stands as a symbol known all over the world, that of a successful international trading company that follows its aims single-mindedly. For the customer, Wal-Mart means you can get a microwave for less than US $30 or a pack of 24 cans of Sam's Choice coke for $3.64 or, perhaps a paradigm for the trading giant, a gallon jar of Vlasic pickled gherkins (contents 3.785 litres) for $2.97. The jar is so big you need both hands to lift it down from the shelf, and with it you are getting not only the nation's number one brand but a year's supply of gherkins for an entire household, a quantity that symbolizes excess, low price and abundance. In a nutshell, Wal-Mart stands for the unmistakable message, 'Demand more for less!' The DVD player for US $29 is probably Wal-Mart's crowning achievement and a strong symbol of Darwinian perfection.

The second axis: the manufacturers – China and the possibilities of global sourcing

While Wal-Mart is the largest trading company in the world, China represents the biggest manufacturer. It was Napoleon who warned that China is a sleeping giant we should beware of waking. Well, now this giant is stirring in its sleep and poised – as Napoleon correctly predicted – to shake the world. We have become accustomed to seeing the USA, Europe and Japan as the so-called triad and to seeing the economic decisions made in these geographical areas as the most important for the global economy. Today, we realize that China has the potential to become the most important supplier in many widely varying sectors. As a result of its sheer size alone, the removal of trade barriers over the next few years and its growing economic and political power, China will, even in the most conservative estimates, gain more and more in importance in the world of politics and business. The bulldozer metaphor that applied to Wal-Mart on the retailer side applies to China on the supplier side.[1] 'Already, China is emerging as a source of global brands, just as Japan did 40 years ago.'[2] With Chinese brands such as Legend for IT products and computers, Haier for appliances, TCL for mobile phones or Tsingtao for beer – 'Made in China' truly is in the same position today as Japan was 40 years ago, with an immeasurably greater hunger for success and an immeasurably greater potential from the cost point of view and with much greater advantages in the field of import and export policy.[3]

If we take a look at this from the point of view of trade, one cannot possibly overestimate this development in China. In 2002, the world's largest trading company, Wal-Mart, bought goods worth over US $12 billion from China. This already represents over 10 per cent of the USA's $110 billion total imports from suppliers, and in 2003 the figure rose to US $15 billion. For the USA as a whole, China overtook Mexico as number one supplier in 2002, as wages in China are still only a quarter of those in Mexico. The outcome of the competition between the big retailers – alongside Wal-Mart, there are Carrefour, Metro and Tesco – over the role they play in the global league will probably depend on the success or failure of the business relations they establish as retailers and buyers on the Chinese market.[4] The big retailers dictate the rules, and they do their sourcing directly. They no longer need intermediaries who just push up prices. Even though one should never underestimate the importance of the time and politics factors in China, Tony Lisanti is probably correct in his assessment of the situation for the big-league retailers: 'The battle for dominance in China will redefine the meaning of global retailing.'[5]

The extremely high global sourcing figures could even rise a little as a result of marginal phenomena. One seemingly banal example is viniculture in China. In 2003, the area under cultivation for wine increased by 38 per cent to 260,000 hectares compared with 2002. That is already half the size of the area dedicated to this use in Australia, a giant among the wine-producing countries![6] Even if the quality – as is the case with many other products – does not yet meet European standards, and even if there are no outstanding brands yet, the export potential is gigantic. The Chinese have already cut back their imports from Chile – home-grown wine is much cheaper. And we must never forget that the Chinese have time and that they have always been very willing to learn (impatience is a Western phenomenon and predominantly a US one). A typical indication of the situation of the middle classes is wine consumption. When the consumption of hard liquor (whisky, brandy etc) falls and tastes become more differentiated, the interest in wine increases. This is already the case in China today. Wine is of symbolic significance for consumption and consumer behaviour in a country, as we have seen very clearly in the USA over the past decades.

Or, to take another example, why should the Chinese leave the automobile market to groups like VW, General Motors or Toyota? In 2002, the first 252 Chinese-built cars were shipped to the USA. Selling price: US $6,000, fuel consumption under 4 litres per 100 kilometres, and the car is called the Xialis.[7] Of course this prototype is not yet ready to take the USA, let alone the pampered European car market, by storm. The infrastructure for the supply system is much too diffuse, the production plants are much too small and the roads outside the urban centres too bad. But let us not forget that a Korean manufacturer like Kia took only 10 years to produce cars acceptable to US customers, and Hyundai has been a success story in Europe. Why shouldn't the Chinese achieve just as much? Why should they be content to export cars only to their already established markets? Will their pride allow them to do so?

There will also be bitter competition within the Chinese market itself. With a population of 1.4 billion, sourcing will be a gruelling marathon with the motto 'Survival of the cheapest'. Chinese companies that have begun to establish themselves as exporters over the last few years are now complaining of rapidly eroding margins. The pressure to lower prices immediately becomes stronger, as you can always find even cheaper suppliers within China. One example is the Ching Hai Electric Works Co, which produces white goods. Because giants like Wal-Mart are fishing these waters, the wholesale prices for ventilators or toasters have fallen from US $7 10 years ago to US $4 today.[8] The pressure on manufacturers to streamline has become stronger and stronger since the liberalization of the markets. Salaries are well below the required local minimum. Ching Hai pays US $32 a month, which is 40 per cent below the local requirements. Young, unskilled workers often earn barely 1 dollar a day. An 18-hour working day is not unusual. Redundancies are becoming common in China, too. At the same time, the average profit margins have dropped from 20 per cent to 5 per cent over the last 10 years. Not even the loosest code of conduct for suppliers is really adhered to. Because the Chinese are so bent on achieving economic growth, they frequently ignore even the minimum standards – hygiene at work, monitored working hours, safety regulations and a minimum of training for a workforce from a largely agricultural background. The pressure to get on and to earn money seems to take priority over all sensible limitations on sustainable development. And the big-league retailers are ready and waiting to profit from it.

We can safely assume that Chinese products, which are perhaps of only modest quality today, will increase continually in quality in the coming years and become attractive as branded goods for export to the Western nations. In many areas, we will have even more overcapacity in the West – which will force us to be even more flexible on prices. That globalization is a blessing for China (and for the Chinese government) is also emphasized by leading experts on China.[9] Growth and prosperity are goals towards which the Chinese are striving with great single-mindedness, endurance and discipline, and above all these are goals prescribed by the political leaders. If this development follows a reasonably stable course, China will establish itself on global markets as a cheap manufacturer, it will prosper and its people will reap the rewards long since reaped by those in the West, while any attempt to block this development politically will frustrate the people and increase the danger of instability.[10]

The third axis: the customer – the internet and the global customer cartel

The last few years have taught us a few things: what the New Economy symbolizes, or what represents the greatest benefit for the customer, is being able to get better and better information more cheaply than ever before. The internet is primarily not a sales channel, but an information channel that empowers the customer. There is a very good book on this subject, *The Cluetrain Manifesto*,[11] but unfortunately its publication passed unnoticed in the turbulence of media hype and the bursting of the bubble. Its main message is that markets are becoming dialogues and it is easier and easier for people to communicate with each other. And they can react swiftly and assert themselves against businesses where the need arises – Smart Mobs is the watchword.[12]

This means increased transparency, and it becomes much easier to exert pressure on companies that treat their customers badly. However, this also means that customers are trained to take a more active, even aggressive, role. Slowly but surely, they increase their expectations of the products and services a company provides, and they will demand that these expectations are met. Why should I pay more for a product from Supplier A when I can get the same quality at a lower price from Supplier B? It's more and more difficult for companies to defend themselves.

If we look at the three axes together, we see that we can apply Leo Strauss's famous phrase 'retail sanity but wholesale madness'.[13] Wal-Mart is passing the enormous pressure back to the supplier (or to the wholesale trade, of which Wal-Mart is increasingly independent). Is it not logical then that the customer should pass the pressure back to the retailer?

An important question will be: where will alliances be formed? The way things are going, the manufacturing side should be feeling the heat most. But we should not underestimate them – think of the food and near-food giants. Will the customers accept a Wal-Mart that dictates the pace? And who are the winners anyway? Who are the losers? Is it possible that all three parties might be on the winning side? Or only two of them? Or none at all?

From a purely theoretical and very simplified point of view, the following variations are conceivable:[14]

Manufacturer + Retailer ➜ Customer	Under the leadership of the manufacturer, the retailer and the manufacturer dictate what the customer gets.
Retailer + Customer ➜ Manufacturer	Under the leadership of the retailer, the pressure on the manufacturer is increased.
Manufacturer + Customer ➜ Retailer	Under the leadership of the manufacturer, an attempt is made to bypass the retailer completely and communicate directly with the customer.
Customer ➜ Manufacturer + Retailer	With the help of new channels (especially mobiles, the internet), the customer exerts pressure on the manufacturer and the retailer.

The pendulum is swinging in the direction of the final consumer. As described above, there is historical proof of this. But in our complex, dynamic and increasingly global economies and society, it is far from certain who will play the decisive role in the axis of evil or the axis of good and for how long.

Which factors are accelerating the trend?

Let us summarize the most important factors.

Liberty, equality, money – political and democratic causes

As the process of democratization moves forward, there is less and less that distinguishes us (because all values are individually selected) except money. We are free, we have equal rights and we need all our financial resources to realize our freedom and our equality. This means that the price also becomes more and more important in our political institutions. Whether political programmes are a success, whether political projects can be realized, is increasingly a simple question of price. The motto of the French Revolution always had more trouble with the third link in the chain, *fraternité*, that is fraternity. And today we can see that, under changed conditions, none of the terms we could substitute for fraternity will work either. Solidarity, for example, only works as long as there is a vast population of young people able and willing to support the smaller group of older people, or if economic growth is sufficient to finance ideologies. If we take a more realistic look at things and leave aside political slogans, we have to admit that money should replace fraternity in the list.

The deterritorialization of competition – economic rationalization

A world that is increasingly linked via internet and IT allows small and medium-sized companies to participate on global markets under more favourable conditions, provided that they can carve out a niche for themselves. In the case of the larger companies, we can see that the more mature, the richer, the more saturated the markets are, the more economic modernization will also mean increased price orientation, because the increasing liberalization and deregulation of the markets – even where it is accelerated by crises, re-regulation or catastrophes – also brings more deterritorialized competition. Large companies, especially if they are stock market listed, have no other choice but to expand into foreign markets. Would Wal-Mart, which until recently sold itself to its customers as a typical US enterprise ('Buy American!'), ever have expanded its operations abroad without the pressure to provide increased shareholder value? Of course, it is true that any company that has acquired the corresponding skills and an appropriate capital basis through economies of scale on the domestic market will have to expand abroad sooner or later. But a smaller company – as we have seen in the food service sector – takes a smaller risk than a large-scale provider such as Wal-Mart. And so we can conclude that, as far as expansion into foreign markets is concerned, the discounters offer the most rational business model for the coming years, irrespective of economic fluctuations. They are less vulnerable with their cost structure: they have important costs such as IT and personnel firmly under control and they are therefore strategically more flexible, can implement decisions more quickly and are economically more adaptive. The most impressive example of this is perhaps the cut-price airlines. Deterritorialization means the intensification of competition.

Shrinking populations in the First World – demographic time bombs

With the exception of the United States of America, we in the richer countries are facing the grave phenomenon of dwindling population figures. In Old Europe, migration predominantly affects unskilled work in the service sector, work that is now carried out by people from ever more exotic cultures. We can assume from this that it is going to become more and more difficult to boost demand. While the generation of baby-boomers grew up with inflation and rising prices, Generation X and Generation Y are learning that prices are falling and deflationary tendencies are normal in many fields. All you have to do is wait, and things will be even cheaper! Japan can be seen as the test laboratory for this development, a country from which Old Europe could learn a lot. As an insular nation that over previous centuries learned to live in cultural independence and isolation, Japan in the last 10 years has seen economic stagnation, real-estate crises, structural problems in banking, deflationary tendencies in many product areas and an advanced ageing of its population.

It seems unlikely that we can rely on the capital factor as a motor for growth over the next few years. Who is going to be prepared to invest in national economies in Old Europe where the population figures are going to shrink in the coming decades – unless, of course, people change their ideas about family planning radically and soon? It seems more likely that, with time and almost unnoticed, Europe will become a kind of glorious museum where we permanently celebrate our past: our political and cultural history together with the art and the religion of past centuries – Venice is one of the possible models here.[15]

White-collar offshoring – the migration of high-quality services to low-wage countries

The outsourcing of increasing sectors of production from the First to the Second or Third World means increasing pressure on prices, and not only in the case of simple products such as textiles or household articles. Nowadays the pressure is felt further up in the value creation chain, in the region of exclusive services.[16] The offshoring of medical expertise, research, chip design, software programming or financial services such as equity research is already in full swing. Why, for example, shouldn't we outsource medical services to India wherever possible if this enables us to keep costs in our health-care system low? Why should the computer analysis that decides whether I need an operation or not be carried out in Germany or Switzerland when I can get the same quality much cheaper elsewhere? A young, well-trained Indian researcher with a university degree costs eight times less than a colleague with the same qualifications in Germany, France or the USA.

And we see the same picture if we compare the services of a senior researcher. The outsourcing potential is vast. Work in this sector could be done not only in India, but also in China, Malaysia, Singapore or South Africa. In the financial services sector alone, various studies and projections indicate that, of the 13 million jobs in the more mature markets of the USA, Europe and Japan, around 2 million are likely to have been outsourced to the Pacific area by 2008.[17] And Heinrich von Pierer of Siemens said of software development: 'For the same money it takes to hire 2,000 German software developers, I can get 12,000 in China.'[18] In this branch, it can already be said that 'You see and feel no difference between one of our mobile phones from Kamp-Lintfort and one from Shanghai.'[19]

This means that, if high-grade jobs, not only unskilled or easily replaceable ones, are going abroad, it becomes more and more unlikely that we in the highly developed, more mature countries can rely on the labour factor to drive growth in the coming years.

And on the other hand, we can see that the people of the Western world are less and less prepared to render services of an unskilled nature. The implicit message is: that's work for immigrants. In the countries exporting labour to us, this trend triggers an increasing lack of the so-called love services, which are mainly carried out by women:[20] nannies, cleaners, providers of erotic services, nursing staff – these are the jobs that are exported. Every year, millions of women leave countries like Mexico, the Philippines or Sri Lanka to work in households, brothels, nursing facilities and restaurants in the First World. This does give women in the First World more individual freedom, but at the same time it means an increasing lack of labour in the countries from which these love service providers come.

Re-globalization – globalization works!

Globalization has arrived – not quite as easily as the leading consultants would have had us believe at the end of the 1990s, but nevertheless in a very robust and continual development.[21] It cannot be denied that there will be setbacks again and again, above all in connection with power-political developments. The WTO has its work cut out, and the Cancun summit in autumn 2003 provided an indicator of all the coming problems. Dictators, fundamental ideologists and other fanatics may slow things down temporarily, but once the Age of Cheap and the desire to get a slice of the action have been awakened, they cannot simply be made to go away again. It is uncertain how far the up-and-coming nations – for example China or Russia – will succeed in achieving a sustainable prosperity that does more than simply feed new oligarchies, but it is, on the other hand, quite certain that the distribution of wealth in today's rich nations is going to change again. And increasing unrest and the potential for conflict between nations – consider terrorism – means less peace of mind, which is a further topic that will dominate in the years to come. Cheap and easy access to information also makes it easier to engage in terrorist activity. In the Age of Cheap, warlike activities also become cheaper: we have discount wars in the double sense.

The fact that engaging in warlike activities is becoming cheaper demonstrates more effectively than anything else how competition is increasing in the economy and trade while, at the same time, we have less and less peace of mind. In the Cold War, we had the immense economic and socio-political advantage of an age of civil peace in that we were able to externalize our conflicts. Now we have exactly the opposite situation. While conflict is hardly possible between the saturated countries – just take Europe, with the exception of the potential crisis area of Kosovo, as an example – our interest moves to civil insecurity: never before have so many countries been potential targets for acts of terror or warlike activities. That means that our power-political situation resembles that of Ancient Rome. Even though the Americans are indisputably the number one military power and in spite of all their advanced technology and their vast financial and personnel resources, there is no way they can guarantee world peace.

The IT revolution – price consciousness is on the increase

The fact that information is easier and easier to acquire and at increasingly low cost further fuels competition. Everyone wants to participate in our economic prosperity. In a connected world, it is no longer possible to hide. As they arise, new opportunities become available to all players on the market at the same time. It remains to be seen whether the Next Big Thing that the Americans are so eagerly anticipating really will arrive and, if so, when. But if there is not a pretty strong kick from the IT sector soon, the situation is going to get much more difficult. And even if we do believe in technology cycles, another quantum leap in the IT sector will undoubtedly also mean rationalization and thus the destruction of existing jobs. And it is unlikely that the end result will be qualitative and quantitative progress.[22] The fact that salaries have been stagnating for some years, coupled with rising unemployment and the – possible – occurrence of economic growth without the creation of new jobs (so-called jobless growth), is likely to reinforce the trend towards lower prices.

The pressure for continual optimization of individual risk allocation

When calculating and deciding whether to take risks or not, what counts for the individual is personal survival. Large-scale risks such as meteorological catastrophes or terrorist attacks on skyscrapers may seem more imminent than ever, but as a risk for the individual they are perceived as less threatening as they increase in scale and frequency. The survival of the individual, and making that survival as comfortable as possible, is much more real. The less the state and companies can guarantee security, the more the onus is on people to take care of themselves. And thus they are more interested in a more personal form of business organization: the insourcing of the familiar. When the welfare state is in a process of reprivatization, it is natural that people want to spread their risks and get rich as quickly as possible. You need money to be able to hoard for the future. And so the aim is for everyone to do his or her own individually controllable risk management. But how should people invest their money? And in what? In gold again? In bonds? Should I invest in funds? Or shares? These all involve a high risk. Not many people believe that we are going to see a stock market boom such as that experienced in the second half of the 1990s in the next few years. Should people put their money in real estate? The example of Japan shows us what that might bring. All these are indications that the pressure on the individual is going to increase.

And our willingness to consume? There's not really much potential – at a high level, of course – for stimulating further growth here, due to a loss of trust. Perhaps this is even the most important argument: the more trust and loyalty are eroded, and the more scandals give the consumer the feeling that suppliers are all out purely to make more money, the more ground the discounters will gain. The 'American Dream' is indeed becoming cheaper, but it no longer has the strength and the inspiration it had in the previous few decades.

An ageing Western society is also more pragmatic, harder to instil enthusiasm into than a society where the age pyramid is reversed. The more we become a society of 'singles', the fewer children we bear, the more dramatic the future psychological crisis will be. There is no rational reason for those who have no descendants to invest in the future. Why should they? Families or, to put it more simply, couples with randomly conceived or, to put it in even more basic terms, randomly produced children have a variety of reasons to have faith in the future. Logically, they want their children to have a good life;[23] they want to be able to spend quality time with their children or simply to have some money to leave to them when they die.

The dream becomes cheaper – the bulldozer rolls on

Finally, let us not forget that there are further, deeper reasons for the Age of Cheap. From 1945 to 1989, we had the two contrasting systems in Germany and the West (Continental Europe). This was in fact what really made the development of the welfare state with its many benefits, possible in the first place. It cannot be denied that its many benefits only arose as an alternative to another ideological system and not simply out of the goodness of the politicians' hearts. From this situation arose a historical compromise, an important stabilizing factor between politics and the economy.

And now we see that, when the system against which the West was competing was removed in 1989, this also removed its motivation to finance the welfare state. And unfortunately, its economic prospects are at the same time overshadowed by falling population figures and the fact that the next leap in technological development is overdue. Continual economic growth in the Cold War was underpinned ideologically. Now, our desire for growth is fed solely by the motivation of the markets to generate prosperity. Ideological motives have evaporated or dwindled to individual concerns. Growth for its own sake is weak, especially in an ageing culture, and is not sustainable. Politicians are at a loss as to how to deal with the problem.

The important question will be: can we stop the bulldozer, and do we want to? What is the price of letting it roll on? What is the price we pay if we stop it? Who can halt it and how without violating basic rights in a liberal democracy?

In the end, we are all probably condemned to consumer democracy and thus to suffer economic and social rationalization. Peace among people and among nations always means that a certain material basis is a given. The period between 1945 and 1989 in Germany taught us that. The social and material security that was created then as a historically necessary compromise between politics and the economy is now being eroded and responsibility delegated back to the individual.

The bulldozer is at the same time both good and evil, bringing as it does both prosperity and its opposite. On the one hand we have Wal-Mart's low prices, the endless variety of products made in China and access to all the information we desire on the internet. On the other hand, we have started to turn a screw that is pushing the great majority of people downwards. When prices are low, wages are also low. When wages are lower, we are more dependent on lower prices. For many of the emerging nations, the situation is on the whole better than it is for the old-established nations of the West with their saturated markets and poor motivation. These traditional markets have, to a large extent, taken on a museum-like character. If the central message of our modern era is indeed, as Turkish social scientist Nilüfer Göle wrote, that we allow the freedom of seduction to dictate our actions,[24] then discounters can look forward to a brilliant future. Everyone can dream, but at a different price.

Notes

[1] One of the first good basic overviews in the rapidly growing flood of publications about the consumer-driven change on the Chinese market is Conghua Li (1998) *China: The consumer revolution*, Deloitte & Touche/John Wiley, Singapore.

[2] John Quelch, 'The return of the global brand', *Harvard Business Review*, August 2003, pp 22–23, 23.

[3] I am also indebted to Mike Moore, the former New Zealand prime minister and head of the WTO, for many interesting insights into China.

[4] In 2002, Carrefour bought goods to the value of around US $1.6 billion from China and, according to the *Wall Street Journal Europe*, 14–16 November 2003, p A6, that figure had already risen to US $2 billion by 2003.

[5] 'Wal-Mart has edge in China battle', *DSN Retailing Today*, 28 October 2003, p 13.

[6] See Jancis Robinson, 'China's middle class leave spirit of revolution behind', *Financial Times*, 11–12 October 2003, p 22.

[7] See Ted C Fishman, 'Here comes the discountmobile', *New York Times Magazine*, 23 September 2003, pp 68–70.

[8] See Peter Wonacott, 'China's factories compete – with each other', *Wall Street Journal*, 14–16 November 2003, p A6.

[9] Michael Yahuda from the London School of Economics. See also Michael Yahuda (2001) 'WTO: China's entry ticket to the international economy', in *Hakluyt*, Hakluyt and Co Ltd, pp 18–22; Michael Yahuda (2000) 'China: Incomplete reforms', in *Towards Recovery in Pacific Asia*, ed G Segal and DSG Goodman, Routledge/ESRC Pacific Programme, New York; Mancur Olson (2000) *Power and Prosperity: Outgrowing communist and capitalist dictatorship*, Basic Books, New York.

[10] If development is relatively stable, China will develop from a manufacturer to a consumer nation. And that will trigger the real revolution.

[11] Christopher Locke *et al* (2000) *The Cluetrain Manifesto: The end of business as usual*, Perseus, Cambridge.

[12] See Howard Rheingold (2002) *Smart Mobs: The next social revolution*, Perseus, Cambridge. The strength of Rheingold's books lies in the fact that they always focus on the social aspect of information and communication and then consider applications. This was a weakness of many interesting approaches to virtual communities at the turn of the millennium; see for example John Hagel III and Arthur G Armstrong (1997) *Net Gain: Expanding markets through virtual communities*, Harvard Business School Press, Boston, MA.

[13] Philosopher Leo Strauss said this in connection with political systems – the health produced on the one side causes the disease to break out on the other.

[14] I hope the wholesale trade will forgive me for reducing the subject to just three stages in order to simplify things.

[15] See also the section on Venetianization in Chapter 4.

[16] See the 2003 Special Edition of the *McKinsey Quarterly*, in particular 'Offshoring and beyond' by Vivek Agrawal *et al*, pp 24–35, and 'Who wins in offshoring', pp 36–53.

[17] See, for example, Dan Roberts and Edward Luce, 'Service industries go global: how high-wage professional jobs are migrating to low-cost countries', source Deloitte Research, in *Financial Times*, 20 August 2003; also, with special focus on India, Justin Fox, 'Where your job is going', *Fortune*, 24 November 2003, p 50.

[18] Interview in *Der Spiegel*, 'Genug geredet', No. 42/2003, pp 48–50, 50.

[19] Source as quoted above.

[20] See the impressive book by Barbara Ehrenreich and Arlie Russell Hochschild (eds) (2003) *Global Woman: Nannies, maids and sex workers in the New Economy*, Metropolitan Books, New York.

[21] I will refrain from giving an overview of the over-optimistic and lyrical publications on the subject of globalization in the second half of the 1990s. On the other hand, more recent publications, those of the last two or three years, are over-pessimistic, a sign of the deep scars left by various acts of terror.

[22] The next really big development will probably be the biotechnological revolution. And that is not likely to take place in the next few years. A lot of legal paperwork will have to be done before it can reach its full potential.

[23] This, by the way, is another reason why well-functioning family businesses probably do have a future. A family business naturally deals with capital and company interests in a way that is different from that of a company that is driven by shareholder value alone.

[24] See Nilüfer Göle (2002) 'The freedom of seduction', *NPQ New Perspectives Quarterly*, **19** (1), Winter, pp 71–78.

3 The Wal-Martization of our society

How we are all becoming Wal-Mart[1]

Excess, superabundance and rock-bottom prices are part of the same phenomenon. They are the logical counterparts to an ascetic form of business management: be faster, better, cheaper. They are also the quintessential expression of the paradox of globalization. The pressure of shareholder value, or to put it more generally of today's financial markets, means on the one hand that management salaries have reached a level that to some arrogant consultants might seem justified, but that in the light of plain common sense seems unreasonable. The same can be said of the excesses in the downward spiral in discounting: if you are right at the bottom of the wage hierarchy, you will never earn decent money, no matter how fast you run. On the contrary, you will need low prices because your wages will fall. To understand Wal-Mart is to reach a basic understanding of an economy that is in the process of becoming global.

Why Wal-Mart concerns us all

Business schools make their money by continually tracking down new success models in business life and then teaching them in courses. Thus they teach students what real success is. The more a company is considered a model case, the more likely it is to be the subject of a so-called case study today. And if the big business schools use your company as a case study, all the other schools immediately follow suit. What Harvard or Stanford or INSEAD offer will be taught immediately all over the world, from Singapore to Dallas to Manchester. Case studies are rituals every student has to go through today. Traditionally, it was mainly the big US industrial groups and their development, for example General Motors or General Electric, that were among the favourites worldwide, and the case 'Polaroid versus Kodak' was one of the classic case studies. However, the last five years have seen a change. For a long time, retailers were not taken seriously and university chairs for retail trade were rare. Hardly anyone paid them much attention. But now the retail trade has become the focus of attention. The Harvard Business School now sells Wal-Mart case studies to other business schools all over the planet – Wal-Mart has become a bestseller! In March 2003, an in-depth study of the strategy of neighbourhood markets was published, ie the strategic expansion of the Wal-Mart model that declares war on the smaller local chains over shares of the food market. Wal-Mart is the star today, and there is far more interest in Wal-Mart than there ever was in the classics of industry.[2]

Why is this so? For the past hundred years, the power lay with the manufacturers. In the power game between manufacturer, retailer and customer that we described in Chapter 1, the customer didn't come into it and the retail trade played a very subordinate role. It was the manufacturer who had the power and the know-how, particularly in the sector of consumer goods, while the retailer was simply a distributor of goods, often also dependent on intermediaries, a relatively insignificant link in the value creation chain. The great brands of Procter & Gamble, Nestlé and Coca-Cola, on the other hand, have long reached worldwide fame and presence. The distributors of goods needed them in order to reach their customers. This has changed drastically since the 1990s. First of all, the retailers who were traditionally active only at a local or regional level expanded geographically and made a name for themselves at a national level. And over the last few years, a consistent if not always simple process of internationalization has taken place, a process that goes beyond the mere conquest of neighbouring markets. The French Carrefour group was the spearhead, followed in France by Auchan and Casino, in Germany by Metro and in Britain by the late starter Tesco, which is now pushing towards the east. And in the USA, of course, there is Wal-Mart. These companies are all examples of the shift in power in distribution – from the manufacturer to the retailer, a shift that will tend to cut out the intermediary, since the big retailers can buy direct (global sourcing). The question today is: who has privileged access to the customer?

Manufacturer → Retailer → Customer

It is the retailers who definitely have the advantage. They have direct contact with the customer and, over the last few years, have learned how to handle IT systems and how to make better use of the advantages of customer communication. With the help of ECR (efficient customer response), they have steadily expanded their know-how and made themselves more independent of the manufacturers.

Today, Wal-Mart is *the* company to watch for strategy, pricing, logistics, IT, dealing with rivals, relationships with suppliers, cost structure and advertising. The fact that, here, cost cutting is an integral part of company culture may be the most striking. But Wal-Mart is also admired for the fact that it makes markets and that its growth is mainly organic and not simply the result of acquisitions as Ahold's was. Wal-Mart's role is that of a market maker, not simply a market taker.

Of course, Wal-Mart is also talked about because, as a representative of a traditional sector, it has the most amazing growth history and is now gaining in significance internationally and in connection with the battle for globalization. Wal-Mart sells goods we all need. Twenty years ago, the teachers at the business schools ignored Wal-Mart because, in accordance with the will of its founder, Sam Walton, it concentrated on the unsophisticated needs of customers in rural areas, but when the chain expanded into suburban, more prosperous areas hardly anyone could ignore Wal-Mart any more. Moreover, many former MBA students are now among the losers in this expansion process: small, independent retailers in the non-food and more and more frequently also in the food sector were forced to give up when they lost the price battle to the giant Wal-Mart. Nowadays, unlike just 10 years ago, Americans grow up with Wal-Mart – it sells everything you need for everyday life. A further important reason for the high degree of interest is that it is much easier to analyse Wal-Mart than Microsoft or HSBC. The basic principle 'higher value, lower cost, every single day' is their message to the customer. What bank or software company could make that claim?

What is Wal-Martization?

Wal-Mart is a symbol we customers have been trained to react to, which has become such a part of our consciousness that we intuitively and ritualistically call it up whenever we go shopping.[3] Wal-Martization is the dominant model of the rationalization of consumer living today. It is the most consistent embodiment of the philosophy 'faster, better, cheaper' and 'bigger, more global, standardized'. Wal-Mart cuts prices because it can. All the time. And much more – Wal-Mart is an expression of the paradox of a world involved in a process of globalization and liberalization. While we profit as customers from the mountains of low-priced products, at the same time we are accelerating the process of downsizing, which tends towards a system where you have badly paid, unskilled jobs with poor career prospects on one hand and a few extremely well-paid and exciting top jobs on the other – with nothing in between the two. In the USA there is increasing criticism of the fact that Wal-Mart became so successful with the slogan 'Buy American' and by catering to the needs of a rural clientele but is now the biggest promoter of job outsourcing from the USA to Asia. The emotional area of superstores and discount stores provides the clearest example, because it affects such an everyday occurrence as shopping. Wherever Wal-Mart appears on the scene, the landscape changes: economically, socially, culturally. According to Retail Forward,[4] for every Supercenter that Wal-Mart opens in the next two years two existing super-markets will close and disappear from the scene. This makes Wal-Mart the most prominent and authoritative expression of the paradoxical and insoluble link between excess, superabundance and discount.

How does the company see itself? Interestingly, Wal-Mart sees itself first and foremost as a distributor of goods for its customers and not as a retailer. Accordingly, the parameters for success are the low distribution costs it achieves in cooperation with its biggest suppliers. Jay Fitzsimmons, Treasurer of Wal-Mart, says: 'Wal-Mart is not in the retail business, but in the distribution business. It is concerned with getting merchandise from the dock of Procter & Gamble into the trunk of a customer's car in as little as 72 hours. Wal-Mart has the lowest prices because it has the lowest distribution costs.'[5]

Thus, bridging distances efficiently and effectively is at the core of Wal-Mart's success. In the Age of Cheap, logistics is the key. What counts in the end is logistical intelligence, the mastery of routes and a corresponding IT architecture. Everything else follows on from that. A faster turnover of consumer goods, meaning better inventory management with the FMCGs (fast-moving consumer goods), is the basis for success, because fast-moving consumer goods mean fast-moving consumers. If the target today is to get an article from the dock of Procter & Gamble into the trunk of the customer's car within 72 hours, it will be 68 hours tomorrow and 62 hours the day after that. A faster turnaround of goods means a faster turnaround of customers. In other words, the company doesn't simply have the lowest prices because, thanks to the scale of the orders it places, it has the lowest purchasing prices. Wal-Mart has the lowest prices because it has the lowest distribution costs. While Target, one of Wal-Mart's few strong competitors in the USA, also places its focus on efficient supply chain management, it retains an even stronger focus on warehousing and above all on retail trends.[6]

However, as we have already indicated, the Wal-Mart phenomenon does have two sides. We have said that it stands for the paradigm of globalization and deregulation. And globalization and deregulation can only be had with a resulting paradox. While on the one hand customers have a high degree of faith in the company and the basic message of low prices sounds positive, step by step Wal-Mart is destroying not only organically grown trading landscapes, but also social networks. There are websites, case studies and books on this subject, too.[7] The significance and social relevance of Wal-Mart in this area can hardly be overestimated.[8] The company has recognized that it can make best use of its strengths if it concentrates even more on the domestic market and on the neighbouring Canadian and Mexican markets. And then, using the profit thus generated and together with its British base (Asda), it can continue to invest in the global markets, after first exploiting its synergy potential in the USA, for example by creating new distribution channels.

For example, in February 2004, the Grocery Supercenter channel opened, a cross between the well-known General Merchandise Stores (the traditional channel of the discounters) and the Supercenters, which rely heavily on food. It is thus in direct competition with Californian supermarkets like Vons (which belongs to Safeway), Albertsons or Ralphs (Kroger group), which are on average 14 per cent more expensive. This has led to mass protest, as these other chains are only too aware that, in the last 10 years, Wal-Mart has already driven more than two dozen national supermarket chains bankrupt.[9] And they also know full well that this increases pressure on employees to work for lower wages. Whereas the average hourly wage for union-organized employees in California is US $13, Wal-Mart pays a mere $8.50. This amounts to around US $14,000 a year – in California, the poverty line for a family of three is US $15,060. And the social insurance system, for example health insurance, is much worse.

Because of this many employees fear it will bring to an end their modest middle-class standard of living. And in the end, it is the state that is called upon to solve the problems created by the company. Today, young people who (have to) take jobs where they earn only $8.50 an hour have no chances of promotion – in stark contrast to the situation 20 years ago. Today they quit after only a few months. And the pressure is increasing. As wage costs are high in the supermarket branch (Supercenters), cuts are being made in social insurance and, of course, the employers want no truck with the unions. Highest priority is accorded to the philosophy of EDLP – every day low price – or, as Wal-Mart's enemies have it, EDLE – every day low ethics. But since Wal-Mart follows its philosophy so relentlessly, its competitors are forced to string along in order to remain competitive, for at least a little while.

Most economists in the USA argue that the Wal-Martization of labour is simply evidence of a functioning free market economy. They argue that, if Wal-Mart helps its customers to save billions of dollars every year, all its rivals have to follow suit. In this way, US consumers save around US $100 billion per year.[10] This intensifies the paradoxical consequence of globalization and deregulation. 'In this day and age, the United States needs more companies like Wal-Mart to create jobs, even if not at the highest pay. The company that makes its mark by taking the cost of manufacturing products and services up will lose, and the country that promotes that will lose.'[11]

The Wal-Mart phenomenon is of such significance because it carries a symbolic value. It stands paradigmatically for the economic and social trend towards cheaper products and services and it stands for the last 25 years of the US way of rationalizing our way of life. Let us now summarize the most important points.

Everything is about 'price' and 'value' as the motor for development

Wal-Mart may have low prices every day, but that doesn't necessarily mean that Wal-Mart is the cheapest store or even a store whose entire range is cheap. It does not only sell low-priced products, but proceeds from the premise that price and value are increasingly important. What value do I get for what price? Potentially, every product could be included on its list if its value can be made attractive. In other words, Wal-Mart will continue to develop wherever it has something to offer for customers from all levels of society. If Wal-Mart can offer its customers diamond rings for US $100,000 or exclusive Opus One wines from Mondavi for more than $100 a bottle, then it is happy to do so. In 2001, the distribution outlet Sam's Club began offering the prestige wine Opus One for US $114 a bottle – 30 per cent less than the normal retail price. And they also have diamond earrings for US $40,000, and they do sell well, even in such a prosaic environment as that of Sam's Club.[12] And when you see what additional incentives can be generated for the customer, it becomes immediately clear that a new type of shopping experience is being created here.

The customer can choose between the following modes of payment: paying cash or paying with the channel's own credit card. But the traditional big-name credit cards are not accepted! One customer who bought $40,000 diamond earrings was not too happy about this. He wanted to get bonus miles for the sum, a sort of incentive to make such a big purchase at Wal-Mart – free flights to the Bahamas for himself and his wife. How did he solve the problem? He went to the normal Wal-Mart discount store and bought gift vouchers for US $40,000, paying for them with his gold card from one of the big credit card companies, which put the bonus miles on his account. And with the gift vouchers, he went to Sam's Club and bought the diamond earrings.

This example also illustrates that a growing number of customers no longer feel the need to go to Tiffany's or upmarket boutiques where there is an appropriate ambience for the product. The favourable price is more important. And the emotional pull of the low price is such that they are more than happy to do without the sales patter.

In the battle for financially strong but price-conscious customers, Wal-Mart, Costco and Target are always adding new products and ranges. You could say that premium articles are rapidly becoming mass merchandise.[13]

But whichever way you look at it, suppliers on Wal-Mart's list don't have an easy time of it. Wal-Mart – like Aldi – adheres strictly to its own set of principles. They include keeping to agreements, being honest, settling invoices punctually and not cheating. The first effect of such a cooperation is a disciplinary one. In the case of basic products that remain unchanged, Wal-Mart's product policy states that Wal-Mart and the final consumer will pay less for them every year. Suppliers have to adapt to that and fulfil Wal-Mart's requirements; then they have to live with it. For Wal-Mart's approximately 21,000 suppliers, low prices come at a high cost that they have no choice but to accept. Let us return to the example of the pickled gherkins mentioned in Chapter 2. These gherkins are the United States' leading brand, Vlasic. It may be a bargain for customers to get a gallon of best-brand pickled gherkins for only $2.97. But the bottom line is that Vlasic and Wal-Mart earn next to nothing on this product.[14] With the start of this mega-price campaign, Vlasic began to cannibalize itself. Consumers who used to buy their gherkins in the supermarket now buy them at Wal-Mart, because they are far cheaper there. A family eats a quarter or a third of the jar and then has to throw the rest away because they can't possibly eat them all before they go bad. Even if the whole family eats the gherkins, there's no way they can get through all of them in time. The deal has given Vlasic celebrity status on the Wal-Mart shelves, but at the same time the company is forced to buy and produce much more cheaply, as margins have been eroded. Companies like Vlasic that make 30 per cent of their turnover at Wal-Mart are not to be envied. Unless they have done some careful strategic planning, they will run into difficulties. And a supplier that tries to negotiate a higher price with Wal-Mart will very probably be refused and at the same time risks having the rest of its products struck from Wal-Mart's range.

However, the area where most adaptability is required is management. Suppliers that want to work with Wal-Mart have to be leaner, more focused and more efficient. Their whole organization has to be brought into line with these aims. If we look at the power-politics aspect of this, we could speculate that compared with large suppliers – the cooperation between Wal-Mart and Procter & Gamble is the showcase study here – small suppliers are less likely to be in a position to defend themselves against conditions that don't suit them. If they want good growth rates, they have to consider whether they will be able to keep pace with Wal-Mart and its conditions in future. Many cannot resist the temptation to try. And it's not the fault of the retailer. A supplier that loses the Wal-Mart account is going to have to find several new retailers to get anywhere near the same volume of orders. And so it can be said that there's only one thing worse than doing business with Wal-Mart – and that's not doing business with Wal-Mart. If you do business with Wal-Mart, you become a Wal-Mart double. The entire structure and all processes in your company mirror the giant's.

Take the example of Levi Strauss. The giant jeans manufacturer has been having serious problems on all fronts over the last few years, and sales have been falling steadily. Should Levi prostitute itself and crawl to Wal-Mart? The answer is yes, because then it will be forced to bring its chronically unpunctual organization, which almost always delivers late, into line with rigid Wal-Mart standards. What Levi stands to gain by this is volume and attention. The rest, however, could mean the beginning of the end for the brand – look at Vlasic. Wal-Mart expects its suppliers to deliver at prices that are in the lower price segment, unknown territory to Levi Strauss, which has only produced premium jeans so far. The jeans manufacturer finds itself in the bargain basement competing with low-price brands, and experience shows that this is unlikely to result in a strengthening of Levi's higher-priced articles in another channel. Here, too, it is the symbolic significance of the deal that is more important: anyone who enters into a cooperation with Wal-Mart automatically gets an image transfer free of charge. And the new image is unmistakable: cheap. And so one of the icons of US consumer culture closed its last two US production sites in 2003, both of them in San Antonio. Two thousand five hundred jobs were lost, and this once proud company, a company with a well-developed sense of social responsibility, now produces all its goods in Asia and sells them at rock-bottom prices at Wal-Mart. Can there be clearer evidence of the Age of Cheap than the situation of Levi Strauss and Wal-Mart?

In short, Wal-Mart's power over its suppliers is so great that it can find a replacement immediately if they fail to fulfil their obligations. Either Wal-Mart does the job itself (verticalization) or it finds another manufacturer for the product. This means that the supplier's only chance of offsetting its eroding margins is to innovate. This, however, is not a path that automatically guarantees success, because the others will all be trying to do the same thing in order to gain more freedom of action.

The change in the labour force

As described above, this naturally has its effect on a labour force carrying out skilled and well-paid work, as, for example, was typical in the automotive industry. This kind of labour force disappears. Today you can find the same people working on the checkout at Wal-Mart for half the wage.[15]

Many of the more subtle analyses of Wal-Mart were unable to reach a conclusion as to where this development will lead in the end. One thing seems certain: Wal-Mart will have to continue cutting its operating costs. Wal-Mart's wage costs are much lower than those of its competitors, and this is one of the main reasons why its operating costs are also far lower.[16] And so it is hardly surprising that labour relations have clearly deteriorated over the last few years. For many skilled and qualified workers, the fact that they have to work for Wal-Mart symbolizes their failure.

The shift towards a clear separation between a low-cost/low-wage world and a premium world

Shopping at Wal-Mart, people learn that thanks to Wal-Mart they can continue to live their American Dream because the prices are low. A good selection of goods at good prices. But they pay for this with hard work and low wages. And with this logic, it seems inevitable that, if you look closer at the organization, you are going to find it employing illegal immigrants.[17] The downward spiral this causes accelerates.

And this in turn produces the unavoidable double moral standard of a world in the process of globalization.[18] We have a stark contrast between a more and more uncompromising asceticism in working life and utter hedonism in our leisure time, where we have a wealth of inexpensive options. While our work processes require us to exploit our personal resources more and more – time, money, mental and physical energy – in a deregulated world of leisure we get to do whatever we want in our free time. Uninhibited hedonism and inhibited work standards meet in an insoluble paradox.

This Wal-Mart with its low prices (in the sense of value plus price) and its low wages is in an increasingly polarized position in contrast to a world of premium values with exorbitant wages in top management. Here, too, the question is how long this can go on. While the premium prices quickly come under increasing pressure, there isn't really an analogous development with regard to top salaries. If anything, the opposite is the case.

The shift towards standardization and the cheapening of the dream of the 'American Way of Life'

The dream is still there, but it has become standardized and less valuable. It can still be lived, but in a new way, one that changes our lives. According to Marshall Blonsky, Professor at the New School and Parsons School of Design in Manhattan, the culmination of the Wal-Mart way of life today is that it consists of 'America's least common denominators gathered together'.[19] The Wal-Mart stores are not aggressive, but they are soulless and without style. This process of standardization knows no mercy. It relentlessly promotes the highest form of equality among people: 'It [the shopping experience at Wal-Mart] proves something I have been trying to teach for years: the indifferent equivalence of everything with everything else, for an audience that has no concern for that difference, and no discernment of quality.'[20]

In brief, from this perspective too we find a model that subjugates all its activities unconditionally to the tenets of 'faster, better, cheaper'. Perhaps the most interesting consequence of this is that customers forget how to distinguish between the cost of an article and its price. It doesn't matter, as long as the American Dream is cheap. The issue of how it is possible to produce at such low cost and whether, in the end, this makes sense for businesses and for the overall economy becomes blurred.

Shaping leisure and cultural tastes

How do you become a music superstar today? How do you become a movie action hero? How does an author become a best-selling author? It's easy: you just have to get on Wal-Mart's lists. Music experts confirm that the purchasing power of big chains like Target, Kmart or the market leader Wal-Mart also dictates what we do in our free time and sets cultural standards. Without it, country and western musicians like the Dixie Chicks, Toby Keith or Faith Hill would never have achieved star status. And it was mass bookselling and not the modest specialist book trade that made authors like Bernard Goldberg, Ann Coulter, Michael Savage or Bill O'Reilly bestselling authors.[21] Such a development naturally favours the separation of the market into smaller premium segments and the large discount segments. The big retailers and the price clubs have only a very limited range of videos, DVDs, CDs or even vinyl. If it doesn't sell straight away, it is removed from the shelves.

What else is important for Wal-Mart? That there is no cultural deviation. The world's largest trading company has stripped its range of anything that could not be classed as mainstream, for example rapper Eminem's albums or the diaries of Nirvana's Kurt Cobain, which were bestsellers elsewhere. Wal-Mart also

took a Sheryl Crow CD off the shelves because the singer criti-
cized the store on the album for selling guns.

This attitude will of course have immediate consequences for
the production of new titles. 'It is going to hurt the sales of
anything that is at all controversial, and if the stores are not
going to put the CDs on the shelves, then the record companies
are not going to make them,' says lawyer Jay Rosenthal from the
Recording Artists Coalition.[22] In other words, the big retailers
limit the choice their customers have and they only buy from
suppliers who produce hits. The latter are too afraid to criticize
Wal-Mart publicly, because their profits hinge on the big hits.
This in turn determines what we get to see and hear in the traditional trade with leisure and cultural articles. And as Wal-Mart
only takes care of its most important (end) customers, the
process of standardization of the product range is further accelerated – in contrast to Target or Costco, where there is also a
more generous selection of such goods available for customers
with a slightly fatter wallet.

If you take a look at the range of goods on offer in Europe's
hypermarkets, you will see what a pioneer Wal-Mart is here. Its
huge stores with their sales areas of 10,000, 15,000, 20,000
(sometimes even more) square metres have to stock the most
sought-after entertainment products, because a low-price – if
limited – selection of such articles gives customers an important
reason to shop at Wal-Mart again. According to Nielsen Sound
Scan, the big distributors already account for 34 per cent of the
overall US music business's sales to the end consumer, and Wal-
Mart is already at 20 per cent. Many suppliers are forced to
record new versions of their CDs, videos etc to satisfy Wal-Mart's
strict moral standards. All the commonplace stickers you see
today, like 'parental warning', almost unavoidable for hip-hop
music, have to be removed and the offensive song texts wiped.
The result is that many of the larger CD companies in the music
industry have satellites near Bentonville (location of the

Wal-Mart headquarters) so that they are always on the spot to filter out what needs to be censored. Some large companies like Warner Brothers, BMG or EMI even invested in Christian labels for the same reason when there was a hike in the demand for religious music and Wal-Mart decided to improve its service to its customers by catering to it.

This may sound ironic, though it is not intended to. Because the majority of Wal-Mart customers are from a rural, small-town or at most suburban background, we get a distorted picture: trend music like hip-hop or electronic is unnaturally neglected in favour of a mass trend towards country music or Christian-inspired songs such as gospel music. For example, of the total 2.5 million copies of Toby Keith's country CD, 72 per cent were bought from these big distributors and, in the case of the Dixie Chicks, such distributors sold 60 per cent of the total of 7.5 million albums.

In the book trade, the market share of the big distributors and price clubs increased from 9.1 per cent in 1992 to 12.6 per cent in 2002, a fact that is even more surprising when you consider that, owing to its troubles over the last few years, Kmart no longer contributed to this growth. Over the same period of time, Wal-Mart doubled its book sales from 2 per cent to 4 per cent. Typically, the range will encompass fewer than 500 titles and most of them will be paperback. The cover design chosen for a book depends to a large extent on whether it will be Wal-Mart listed. And, as in the music sector, books with a religious/Christian leaning are consciously or unconsciously favoured: large publishing houses such as Crown (Random House and Bertelsmann) or Penguin (Pearson) have launched new product lines to better accommodate this conservative religious trend.

And the same is also true of the growth market in DVDs: 'Wal-Mart now comes close to spending as much on purchasing DVDs and videos as the major studios earn from all the theaters in

America.'[23] This statement was made by former Warner Brothers manager Warren Lieberfarb, who is seen as the father of the DVD.

In the opinion of one of the United States' most influential authors and columnists, David Brooks,[24] Wal-Mart is a projection of the values of the modest middle-class American. 'Wal-Mart knows the value of a dollar. Wal-Mart is patriotic, community oriented, family-centered, rural and religious.'[25] Against this background, it becomes clear why magazines like *Maxim*, *Stuff* or *FMH* have been cleared from the shelves. Topless cheerleaders on the back seats of Maseratis just don't sit well with this world picture. (Although it has to be said that Wal-Mart's attitude is beginning to mirror that of concerned parents in urban areas. Its stores sell a range of condoms, rifles, see-through trousers and cosmopolitan magazines and even a selection of Ozzy Osbourne articles for kids.) The emphasis is on potentially threatening factors, and nothing is allowed to disturb the comforting emotional mood. Exceptions to the rule are made as seldom as possible. Wal-Mart is predictable and security-oriented – an important precondition for growth in these times.

The subtle shift in the significance of media in communication

Wal-Mart is also changing our media landscape. With its 138 million customers per week, the group can be seen as a channel to which the masses tune in every day and might even be said to be first and foremost a centre for mass-media interest. Wal-Mart has the customer completely in its power for as long as he or she is in the store, and so it is not going to waste a moment. Customers have to be taught and bound to so-called patterns of recognition. And in the US consumer landscape today, these patterns have become more important than television, as there is less distraction because the store has direct access to our attention. Although the Americans still hold the international record in average daily television consumption, anyone with an interest in advertising cannot afford to ignore the possibilities offered by the Wal-Mart mass channel.

We can put it like this: the mass channel has replaced the mass media, because the retailer is controller of the time the customer spends in the store. The retailer has the privilege of direct access to the customer. If I'm watching TV, I can zap away from the commercials or even completely programme them out, with the help of the very successful Tivo system, and banish them from the screen. I have no such option with the mass channel. I can't escape the checkout queue. My path from the car park to the frozen goods section of the store is predefined. And a visit to the in-store restaurant is almost inevitable, because by the time I've done my shopping I'm hungry again. And all this means a wealth of opportunities to employ mass media in such stores. Skilful manipulation of the customer with marketing and advertising promises much more success and is much more individual and more personalized than advertising on TV or in the press.

The pioneer of 'faster, better, cheaper' and 'bigger, more global, more standardized' is an economic force to be reckoned with

Larger and larger sales areas, higher turnover, more profit, lower costs, lower prices. It's worth taking a short look at the impressive history of this company from its beginnings in 1962.[26] In 1979, Wal-Mart went public on the New York Stock Exchange. In 1979, it made a turnover of US $1 billion as a discounter. In 1983, the Sam's Warehouse concept was added. In 1988, the first Supercenter was opened. By 1994, there were already 100 of them. By 1995, there were 500 and, in 2001, the 1,000th Supercenter opened its doors. In 1991, Wal-Mart took the plunge and started to operate in Mexico, and from the mid-1990s on it started adding units in countries like Argentina,

Brazil, China, Germany, South Korea and Britain at a rapid, even hasty, pace. The first Neighborhood Market opened in 1998. By 1992, the group employed 371,000 people, by 2000 its workforce exceeded 1 million and by 2008 it will probably have 2.2 million employees.[27] The question that arises is: how long can this go on? The corporate culture of this group is geared to achieving two-digit growth rates every year. So far, this has been possible, in particular in view of the fact that the home market with its population of 280 million holds almost inexhaustible growth potential. By adding new distribution channels, the trade landscape can be revolutionized step by step in almost all relevant product categories.

Wal-Mart really is unrivalled. No other retailer can match these conditions – neither Carrefour nor Metro nor Tesco nor even the bankrupt Dutch Ahold group. They all grew up in much smaller markets. And because of their specialization, stores like Home Depot do not have the same potential for continually integrating new ranges of products and opening new channels. Wal-Mart cannot be topped.

An icon of globalization with the paradox of good and bad

'Americans have decided they want discount shopping in volume, and that's the real world.'[28] On the one hand, this fact makes Wal-Mart the 'most admired' US company, according to an annual survey published by money magazine *Fortune*. But at the same time, this image means that one in three planned new stores will come up against opposition from the local inhabitants. A US market research magazine prefaced its heading for an article on the company with the German words 'Wal-Mart über alles'.[29] What Wall Street sees and praises as 'efficiency' and what meets with the approval of the shareholders are seen as negative by those who see their quality of life impaired by an existing or planned Wal-Mart store in their area. Studies such as that carried out by Professor Kenneth Stone from Iowa State University clearly show the effects Wal-Mart has had on trade and communities in rural and small-town areas over the past 15 years. On the trade side, the bottom line is no gain for anyone except Wal-Mart. When a Supercenter with a sales area of 20,000 square metres descends on a small town like Ankeny, Iowa, which has a population of 27,000, if it generates an approximate turnover of US $75 to 80 million that turnover is simply rerouted from existing trade structures. For the community, the consequences are primarily tax-related: tax revenue falls because, unlike specialist stores and local retailers, Wal-Mart does not reinvest money in the region. Profits are siphoned off to Bentonville. And as the group's organization is more efficient than that of small businesses, it destroys on average 1.5 jobs in rival companies for every new job it creates.[30]

Notes

[1] See also the introductory remarks on Wal-Mart and the 'axis of evil' in Chapter 1.

[2] A look at the following examples will suffice: St Michael's College in Colchester, VT teaches 'Retailing management', with Wal-Mart as the model for trade today. The Cox School of Business, Southern Methodist University in Dallas offers an MBA course entitled 'Operations and technology management', in which Wal-Mart's supply chain management is discussed. The Arizona State University in Temple teaches 'Logistics management' as an undergraduate course in which the main focus is on the use of technology in Wal-Mart's distribution centres. More and more books are being written about Wal-Mart and, whereas until the 1990s interest centred on Sam Walton as its founder, the main question today is how his heirs have handled their inheritance and what happens to a group that is subjected to a process of forced growth and internationalization.

[3] Among the more recent literature on Wal-Mart, see Robert Slater (2003) *The Wal-Mart Decade: How a new generation of leaders turned Sam Walton's legacy into the world's no. 1 company*, Portfolio. The title says it all. The era of Wal-Mart has dawned.

[4]   See Retail Forward's study 'The age of Wal-Mart', August 2002, which gives a very good overview.

[5]   Quoted in *DSN Retailing Today*, 7 April 2003.

[6]   For a good overview and evaluation of Wal-Mart's commercial potential, see the study 'The age of Wal-Mart' by Retail Forward, published in August 2002.

[7]   See, for example, Bill Quinn (1998) *How Wal-Mart Is Destroying America: And what you can do about it*, Ten Speed Press, Berkeley, CA, or the seminar at Centre College in Danville, KY on the subject of Wal-Mart's influence on independent retailers and the agglomeration era of towns and cities.

[8]   See Steven Greenhouse (2003) 'Wal-Mart, driving workers and supermarkets crazy', *New York Times*, 19 October, p 3.

[9]   Source as quoted above.

[10] See also Greg Scheider and Dina ElBoghdady (2003) 'Wal-Mart shapes labor force: U.S. rivals struggle to match savings from retail powerhouse', *Wall Street Journal Europe*, 7–9 November, p A5.

[11] Quote from market researcher Gary Stibel from the New England Consulting Group, source as stated above.

[12] See Ann Zimmerman (2001) 'Très cheap: taking aim at Costco, Sam's Club marshals diamonds and pearls', *Wall Street Journal*, 9 August, pp 1, 4.

[13] See also Constance L Hays (2002) 'Built on working class, Wal-Mart eyes BMW crowd', *New York Times*, 24 February, pp 1, 24.

[14] Apparently, Wal-Mart sells 240,000 gallons a week in the USA, that is 12,480,000 gallon jars a year. The manufacturer and the retailer make just one or two pennies per jar. See Charles Fishman (2003) 'The Wal-Mart you don't know: why low prices have a high cost', *Fast Company*, December, pp 68–80.

[15] See Jim Hopkins (2003) 'Wal-Mart's influence grows: retail giant puts pressure on everything from prices to wages', *USA Today*, 29 January, pp 1, 2.

[16] See Mark Gimein (2002) 'Walton made us a promise: Wal-Mart's founder made a pact with employees: He would be fair to them, and they would work hard for him. It was a good deal, but can it survive in the 24-hour service economy?', *Fortune*, 18 February, pp 67–72.

[17] See Stephanie Armour and Donna Leinwand (2003) 'Feds: 300 Wal-Mart cleaners illegal', *USA Today*, 23 October, p 1, also: 'Eine Schattenseite des UA-Arbeitsmarktes: Wal-Mart beschäftigte 300 illegale Einwanderer', *Neue Zürcher Zeitung*, 25/26 October 2003, No. 248, p 25.

[18] No one has described this better than Daniel Bell (1976) did in his book *The Cultural Contradiction of Capitalism*, Basic Books, New York.

[19] See Marshall Blonsky (1992) *American Mythologies*, Oxford University Press, New York.

[20] This is certainly different in Europe, where strong traditions have encouraged the desire for differentiated tastes.

[21] See David D Kirkpatrick (2003) 'Shaping cultural tastes at big retail chains', *New York Times*, 18 May, pp 1, 21.

[22] Source as quoted above, p 21.

[23] See source as quoted above.

[24] Brooks writes for publications such as *Weekly Standard*, *Newsweek*, *Atlantic Monthly* and *New York Times Magazine*. He is the author of *Bobos in Paradise*.

[25] See David Brooks (2003) 'No sex magazines, please, we're Wal-Mart', *New York Times*, 11 May, p 14.

[26] Firms of consultants often fall over themselves in their eagerness to present their numerous analyses of Wal-Mart. A good study is that mentioned above, carried out by Retail Forward in 2002. See also the Institute for Grocery Distribution (IGD) study on Wal-Mart, *The Wal-Mart Report*, 2003.

[27] Figures as per company records and *DSN Retailing Today* (estimates); see *DSN Retailing Today*, No. 17, 8 September 2003.

[28] These are the words of Maurice Pres Kabacoff from Historic Restauration Inc, a developer in New Orleans who endorses the conservation of grown structures. See Constance L Hays (2003) 'For Wal-Mart, New Orleans is hardly the Big Easy', *New York Times*, 27 April, pp 3 and 11, 11.

[29] 'Wal-Mart über alles: how America's communities lose out after the retailer moves in', *American Demographics*, October 2003, pp 38–39.

[30] See also Constance L Hays, source as quoted above.

4 The models for present-day rationalization

Aldification, McDonaldization, Starbuckification etc

The rationalization models

The Age of Cheap is producing some very strong models leading to economic and social rationalization. As business models, they influence one or more sectors, and they change customer behaviour permanently and far beyond the mere sphere of business. In order to merit true model status, the model must be unique and exemplary. For example, it must change the way we travel or, even better, our very concept of mobility, alter the way we eat or dictate how we spend our leisure time. Furthermore, a model acquires benchmark character, usually beyond the limits of one single sector and internationally. And it has no lack of imitators. What is significant for our discussion is that, today, such models are increasingly also price-oriented models. Truly dominant models will no longer be able to ignore the price factor in future.

Such models are not found in all industries. As a rule, they are not manufacturer models. For example, Toyota is a great example for the automobile industry – but it has not altered our concept of driving or travel. Sony is a successful group in the consumer electronics branch and has a lot of potential on today's converging markets, as does Nokia. But Sony does not really shape our idea of entertainment and no one really knows what course Nokia will take in future, either. In the case of true models, it is a question of much more than simply brands or brand expansion. True models are so strong that they become a way of life, that is, they can have a lasting influence on our thinking and our behaviour. In other words, they have more than just economic relevance; they are of lasting cultural relevance, too.

Alongside McDonald's and Wal-Mart, there is a whole series of other influential models, which we will only be looking at in outline here. The potential of other models is certainly vast, but they have not (yet) reached the degree of prominence and authority of those mentioned here. Ikea is definitely a candidate, as are Amazon, eBay and perhaps even Google in the internet sector. The future may belong to them, but the present does not yet. And it is not at all clear whether the banks will ever succeed in creating a sustainable model that goes beyond the credit card in the field of financial services. Anything is possible in the Age of Cheap.

McDonaldization: shaping the way we eat today (eat faster, waste less time)

In the 80s and 90s, McDonald's was the main company everyone was talking about. Over the last few decades, this fast food giant has expanded, not only within the United States but globally, at a breathtaking and unparalleled pace. With the help of a simple but efficient business idea, which has done a lot to further the franchising system, it achieved a modernization and rationalization of our

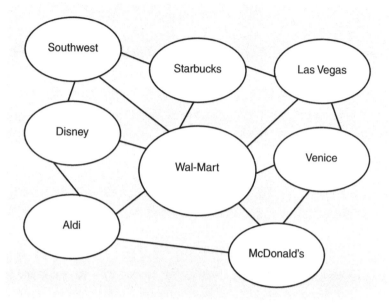

Figure 4.1   Planetary rationalization models

eating culture that is unique in history. McDonald's set many
new standards. For example, new kitchen devices were invented,
the development of new food storage techniques was encouraged, work processes were simplified and new job titles were
devised. McDonald's also made french fries a cult and gave
people who in a capitalist system would otherwise have stood no
chance the opportunity to set up in business.

The most unmistakable sign of McDonald's strength is that it
has become a popular target of attacks by opponents from widely
varying backgrounds. The existence of anti-McDonald's groups
is a clear indication that the company has made it on a global
scale. McDonald's has become the screen on to which health
freaks, anti-globalization theorists, critics of capitalism and
people from other protest movements project their concerns.
This is, of course, of great benefit to the company. We should not
underestimate the fact that, far from damaging its reputation as
the originators intended, vehement protest is actually good for a

brand in the long term (see Nike or Nestlé). For example, and particularly in Europe, sharp criticism has prompted McDonald's to show considerable initiative in sensitive areas such as ecology and supply (buy local). And it is quite remarkable that a US company has been so successful all over Europe. Again and again, McDonald's has found strong personalities for the top jobs in its national organizations. Ironically, McDonald's France, which is run by Denis Hennequin, is one of the most successful and profitable McDonald's divisions, if not the best. If we look at the sum of all these strengths, it is less surprising that McDonald's is the epitome of a modern, international company.

McDonald's has many striking features, although the system is based on very simple principles. In the last 20 years, a McSomething has been created in almost every field. We have had McUniversity, McDoc, McFact, McGolf, McPaper, McHealth, McKids and McFun. The hamburger giant stands for a form of US fast food culture and the American way of life that has long become part of the eating culture of regions all over the world.[1] McDonaldization means that the McDonald's rationalization model is transferred to another sector: it is fast food, snack food, fast throughput and simplification, but also modernity. US social scientist George Ritzer, the author of the most influential books on the McDonald's phenomenon,[2] said some years ago: 'I believe the fast-food restaurant has become the model of rationality.'[3] That may be correct, but events have overtaken this statement.[4] The fast food restaurant has long become a self-perpetuating model, albeit one that, in spite of its overwhelming success, is now fighting not to gather dust.

Let us take a look at the situation in the USA. There are 277,208 fast food outlets in the United States, one for every 1,000 inhabitants, compared with every 1,400 inhabitants in 1990 and every 2,000 inhabitants in 1980. So growth is now looked for where there are most potential customers, namely near Wal-Marts and Home Depots. 'A fast food place is like a fish that follows a shark,' says Michael Howe, CEO of fast food giant Arby's.[5] This means that the further development of the McDonald's model depends to a great degree on whether or not it gains access to the vast markets of the food and non-food retailers and whether it succeeds in adjusting to suit their customers' requirements. In other words, the future of this model will be more and more dependent on the development of other successful models.

The founder of Ikea, Ingvar Kamprad, recognized many years ago just how this dependency works and how to counteract it. The DIY giant with its vast sales areas is all the more successful for having integrated fast food into its concept. 'It is difficult to do business with hungry customers,' he is said to have remarked at the end of the 1950s, thus triggering the launch of Ikea's own fast food division.[6] The main reason why McDonald's is no longer the most influential model of rationalization today lies in complexity. Wal-Mart is able to absorb much more complexity than McDonald's. And today, in an age when the customer's wishes and needs are many and various, this is critical.

Wal-Martification: shaping the way we shop today (or the theme park for every day)

In addition to McDonald's with its lifestyle-creating influence on the way we live today, there is another, even more powerful, model: Wal-Mart. McDonald's advantage lay in offering a highly specialized range of products and in the unparalleled energy with which it proceeded. It redefined food. That is impressive enough, but Wal-Mart is in a different league altogether, taking the development one stage further. It is the model of today. Wal-Mart not only offers a highly specialized service, but it alters our everyday lives full stop. While McDonald's is in the process of entering into the next – difficult – stage in its development, the biggest retail group in the world now faces the task of redefining the business model for the consumer and – as far as possible – introducing it on a global scale. What McDonald's is to the fast food sector, Wal-Mart is to our everyday lifestyle in all activities connected with shopping.

The uniqueness and exemplary character of the Wal-Mart model lies in the fact that it intersects with such a large part of our everyday lives. Wal-Mart is the model of a comprehensive modernization of our lives, a sort of theme park for the things we need every day. In contrast to manufacturer models like Nestlé, Kraft, Procter & Gamble and so on, this retail model can consolidate a very wide selection of offers and take them directly to the customer through its many channels. The very development of its multitude of distribution channels speaks volumes, pinpointing as it does how it is possible to tailor one's activities to target ever-changing customer needs. There are other very strong models, but none of them has such a comprehensive effect.

With Wal-Mart, we are catapulting ourselves into astronomical spheres as far as turnover is concerned. However, the comparison is not perfect. Wal-Mart's annual turnover has reached a dimension where it exceeds that of the GNP of Austria or Turkey. Even for a model that aspires to leading the field in the coming years, such gigantic dimensions are unique. The title of a recent study of Wal-Mart (or rather of Sam Walton's successors, David Glass and today H Lee Scott), *The Wal-Mart Decade*, is probably an understatement.[7] Let me state it again clearly: no other manufacturer or retailer is likely to equal this phenomenon or come anywhere close to attaining such significance in the foreseeable future. Interestingly, however, Wal-Mart is much less original than McDonald's. What Wal-Mart has done was achieved long ago, but to a much lesser degree, by Migros in Switzerland and Leclerc in France and, more recently, by late developer Tesco in Britain. What makes the giant from Bentonville stand out from the rest is the simple fact that it has radically and consistently seized every opportunity the huge domestic market offers and then had the courage, as it became increasingly complex, to slash costs by slashing distribution costs.

Southwestization: shaping our idea of mobility (the archetype of low-price air travel)[8]

Southwest invented cheap flights in the USA over 30 years ago, thus inaugurating an unprecedented increase in mobility that seems to be setting the standards for the industry in Europe, Australia and Asia.[9] Cheap flights means transporting passengers over long distances efficiently and effectively: safety, speed, time gain and comfort.

Where consumer democracy, freedom of choice and low prices are concerned, travel – and especially air travel – holds a particularly privileged position. Unlimited mobility and an ever-increasing number of ways to spend our free time by discovering new countries and regions – what could be more democratic? The travel sector and thus the low-price airlines are probably the real driving force behind the Age of Cheap today – perhaps even more so than Aldi or Lidl. Cheap travel means that we can see more of the world while spending less. Travel, which was once the privilege of aristocrats and until recently a matter of prestige and pride, has now dwindled to a mere commodity. And more than that: travelling has become synonymous with freedom, but – a further paradox – travel is also increasingly the fate of those in search of work. Cheap travel sugars the pill. The wonderful saying 'There is no place like home' expresses in its ambiguity what mobility-hungry and mobility-weary travellers feel today.

Southwest, founded by Herb Kelleher and Rollin King in 1971 and based in Dallas, is indisputably the role model and has reached a size and status that are unique in the airline business. Southwest, with its fleet of 377 planes, all Boeing 737s, is the only important US airline that remains consistently in the black. The only thing that is surprising about the fantastic story of this company, from its foundation to the present day, is why it took its imitators so long to roll out similar models. It is astounding that it was only after numerous crises in the industry that Ryanair was set up in 1985, the start of a new era in which realistic replaced romantic air travel in Europe. Even through the crisis following 11 September 2001, the company continued to make a profit. It is worth more than the other five big national carriers, and with over 64 million passengers every year easily bigger than Lufthansa or British Airways. Today we can see that this model, the embodiment of mass transit operations US-style, is also gradually transforming European travel culture and geography.

Southwest, too, is not really a revolutionary model, but it is a consistent one. The complexity of the airline industry with its many plane types and its many classes of travel with varying service levels and standards of customer treatment is reduced to a minimum here. Southwest no longer tries to do everything for everybody, but concentrates instead on a clearly defined, simple range of services. Southwest could be termed 'the Aldi of the skies'. Its closest imitator is probably Ryanair, which is more consistent than easyJet or other followers like Germanwings or Virgin Blue. 'Ryanair is doing in the airline industry in Europe what Ikea has done. We pile it high and sell it cheap,' says founder and CEO O'Leary.[10] It is certain that easy booking via the internet kicked off the development in Europe. EasyJet and the entire easy philosophy would not have been possible without the internet, and the mathematical leeway offered by yield management has definitely led to a perfectioning of the business in the last few years.

Starbuckification: shaping our idea of convenience today (take a break from the hustle and bustle and enjoy good coffee)

Starbucks is a very exciting example in that, in just a few years, it has managed to reinvent the McDonald's fast food idea and introduce it very quickly all over the world.[11] In just a few years, it created and established a model that stands for a certain lifestyle, which could be described as 'break for coffee'. Howard Schultz took a simple but ingenious basic idea and turned it into a commercial success. There are a lot of stressed-out people who are always on the move, especially in urban areas or other busy places, and these people could do with 15 minutes' break in a pleasant atmosphere. But they will not take that break in their place of work or at home. They go to a third place. And what can you sell customers in 15 minutes? Coffee, or rather a range of coffees. To put it in other words, Starbucks stands for today's idea of convenience. While it would be correct to say that 7-Eleven invented convenience stores, they lack the smart trendy image that Starbucks quintessentially embodies. And the customers pay for that image. Starbucks first revolutionized coffee drinking in the USA and then went on to conquer the Anglo-Saxon countries. The big coffee producers were so busy arguing with the retail chains over shelf positioning, advertising and prices that they failed to notice that Starbucks were creating new customer requirements: a new approach to coffee. Thanks to Starbucks, you can now get a good espresso all over the USA, even in the Midwest and on the highways. In redefining convenience, Starbucks led to an emotional redefinition of coffee and coffee drinking, giving it a lasting image boost and positioning it further upmarket.[12]

However, in a faster-moving society that needs a redefinition of convenience, it is questionable whether the Starbucks model will be as lasting a success as McDonald's. But on a purely symbolic level, Starbucks, too, has achieved a lot – just like McDonald's, Starbucks has become one of the most loved and most hated global enterprises in the world.[13] And to achieve that, you need an extremely strong and valuable brand that reaches mythical dimensions.

We can say that Starbucks is too expensive by the standards of discount and the Age of Cheap, above all in Continental Europe. In Tokyo or Shanghai more than in Dallas or New York, I might feel the urge to escape to a Starbucks and drink an espresso. That gives me a 'global feeling', a feeling of comfort. The price is of secondary importance. But in Berlin, you can drink coffee or espresso in the famous luxury hotel Adlon near the Brandenburg Gate and pay less than you would at the Starbucks on the other side of the street. It is impossible to say how long customers, at least those in Continental Europe, which has its own very varied coffee culture, will be prepared to pay a premium-lifestyle margin. In London, where Starbucks brought about a long-overdue and very welcome revolution in coffee, there is already a price war and the inevitable process of consolidation among operators is in full swing – after a few years when coffee chains were springing up like mushrooms. Hardly any of them, however, has learned how to run a profitable business.

Yet it would be wrong to underestimate Starbucks. It does have great innovative power, and the coffee people from Seattle are extremely active in the sensitive field of customer orientation and the creation of customer loyalty.

Aldification: the hard-core version of Wal-Mart (reduce to the max)

The biggest difference between Aldi and Wal-Mart, apart from the number of products stocked, is that the company from Bentonville has a completely different approach and attitude to IT. While Wal-Mart is the pacemaker in the field of IT, Aldi chose to be a late adopter. As long as you are working with small numbers of different articles, well below 1,000, you can safely rely on the human factor – from the checkout operator to the managing board, everyone knows immediately what articles are popular with customers or why an article is not selling.

Wal-Mart, on the other hand, is dependent on a highly complex information system, which has to be steadily updated to meet changing requirements. When Wal-Mart introduced ECR (efficient customer response) in the 1990s, a process that works best initially with a big supplier like Procter & Gamble or Johnson & Johnson, and then went on to announce in mid-2003 that it would introduce RFID (radio frequency identification) with all its suppliers by 2006, this was bound to have revolutionary consequences for the whole supply chain.[14] Aldi is different: this hard discounter has all the relevant business figures at its fingertips. This is an efficient and effective way to keep complexity manageable. In other words, nothing in the IT field can shake Aldi. When it becomes necessary for them to introduce more advanced technology – for example scanners on the checkouts – they can do so with all the advantages of the late adopter and profit from the mistakes made by their competitors in the field of costs and above all human resources.

Aldi is as German as Wal-Mart is American. Aldi is thorough, consistent and above all – and this is increasingly important in a dynamic and complex world – has remained essentially simple and always refused to follow the popular management or marketing trends.

Even after the fast-paced developments of the 1990s, Aldi remains an intriguing model and should definitely not be underestimated with respect to its further development – but Aldi is also far less complex in its requirements than Wal-Mart. Aldi remains the hard-core discounter, while Wal-Mart, with a range of products that is over 100 times larger, is expected to meet completely different demands. Aldi stands for discipline, German thoroughness, honesty and trust. Add to that abstinence, voluntary narrow-mindedness and attention to detail. But in contrast to Wal-Mart, Aldi is a partial phenomenon. It picks out individual items and has never claimed to satisfy all its customers' everyday needs. Aldi is hard-core. By comparison, Wal-Mart is almost smart.

According to Dieter Brandes, former Aldi manager and proposer of simplicity on all management levels, a consistent reduction to the essentials – and therefore simplicity – is the basis of the Aldi success model: no central admin departments (marketing, controlling, human resources, organization), no benchmarking, no budgets or annual plans, but also resistance to the temptation of making a quick additional profit wherever this would require a deviation from the company philosophy.[15] Common sense, intuition, experience and straightforward organization are the success factors in its management. It follows that Aldi's shoplifting figures are negligible.[16] Aldi also has the advantage of never promising too much. Aldi attaches no added value to making promises to its customers. Customers know what they are getting.

Aldi has the great advantage, from the point of view of its much smaller sales area and more limited range of products alone, that the customer feels more at home there. Aldi can usually be found not far from its customers' homes. In contrast, Wal-Mart's big boxes look threatening and cold, surrounded by their endless car parks. But both companies manage to split public opinion. Like Wal-Mart, Aldi is praised by some and damned by others. As we have already seen in the case of McDonald's and Starbucks, a successful model will have the power to polarize opinions.

On the whole, however, we are probably more disposed to be sympathetic towards Aldi than Wal-Mart. If you talk to customers or businesspeople about Wal-Mart, you will certainly feel a sense of pride and respect for the giant retailer, but on the whole the relationship is a very rational and pragmatic one. The relationship between Aldi and its customers and business partners seems to be of a more emotional nature, which is probably a result of its low-tech image. Wal-Mart is an unfeeling machine that mows down everything in its path. Wal-Mart uses high-tech to monitor everything. At Aldi on the other hand – even if it is for reasons of cost – there is more emphasis on the human factor. That holds true above and beyond the myth of the fastest check-out operators in the world who know all the prices off by heart. If you click through the fan pages on the internet, you can see how essential it is for German consumers to be able to compare mattresses from Aldi and from Norma directly and then to make their findings public. It is almost a declaration of love. We also learn how much time and energy people are prepared to devote to finding out whether it is better to buy their inflatable airbed from Aldi Süd or Tchibo, and that the debate on whether Aldi's electrical goods are better than Lidl's has taken on a dimension similar to that of the ideological dispute in the Cold War. In an e-mail in the discount forum, Thomas writes:

> Hi everybody! Why does Aldi have this cult status? I recently compared Aldi, Lidl, Norma and Penny in the area around my home. In my opinion, Penny leads the field at the moment. Why? If you look at the whole range of consumer goods a normal household needs, it seems to me that Penny has the best range. Glass cleaner, biscuits, descaling sprays, oven lighters etc, etc. No other discounter can offer such a wide range. If I have to do serious shopping for basic household articles, it is usually Penny I will go to. Anyone argue with that?[17]

Or, on the subject of headphones:[18]

> who's got headphones already?
> Author: pepe35
> Date: 14.11.03 09:14
> Hi!
> Has anyone got the stereo radio headphones? What's the quality like?

Answer to this message:

Re: who's got headphones already?
Author: robi
Date: 15.11.03 19:12
Bought a radio headphone set on 7.11 and am very satisfied with the quality. I find them easier to use than the Sony headphones, and they're less than half the price.

Answer to this message:

Re: who's got headphones already?
Author: doggi
Date: 18.11.03 13:55
Bought headphones but will be returning them immediately. Non-stop crackle and frequency range inadequate.

Indeed, more than any other retailer in the world, Aldi has managed to win cult status over the last few decades. Of course, this was not planned. The phenomenon is the result of lucky coincidences, some of which are the result of cleverness on Aldi's part and some due to external influences. On the one hand, the company adheres doggedly to certain principles, and on the other there is the economic climate, which has helped it to attract wider sections of the population, who then become loyal customers of Aldi because of their positive experience with the stores. The majority of Aldi customers today are not poor people. A quote from Oskar Lafontaine from the late 1990s shows how the old ideological picture of Aldi customers has changed: 'Our aim is to relieve the burden on those who shop at Aldi, not those who wear Rolex watches.'[19]

Culturally, it could perhaps be said that the contrast between what is – for example in the eyes of the Swiss – a grotesque and almost spooky penny-pinching when doing one's grocery shopping and the willingness to spend unbelievable amounts on a car is something very German and is probably not found in any other European country. If Wal-Mart is the model of the present and if it is going to maintain its high growth rates in the future or implode under its own weight one day, then we can say of Aldi that here cult status is rapidly becoming classic status. Aldi is the Heidegger of the retail trade. And thus probably immortal.

The only thing Aldi lacks today is the step from cheap to cheap chic. In a fully developed consumer culture, trying to propagate something that has the smell of asceticism will position you more in the field of necessities than of life-enhancing luxuries. Aldi has the romantic flair of the corner shop combined with the discount prices of today. The US cheap chic chain Trader Joe's is much better in this respect – strangely, as already mentioned, it is part of the Aldi group. Aldi – see Lafontaine – stands for poverty, but Aldi also stands for miserliness – see the many bargain hunters greedy to save money there even though they don't need to. Neither of these attitudes brings a positive reinforcement – unless you are a masochist and get a real buzz from shopping in the most unerotic surroundings. Of course, these considerations don't enter into the equation for the discounters. Their driving force is and always has been the same: being cheaper than their rivals.

Cheap chic could also be a way to break the rigid polarization of supermarket/hypermarket and hard discounters in Germany. The defensive attitude of the supermarkets and their naïve belief that they can force the manufacturers of branded articles to quote them better prices and conditions than they do the discounters fails to address the real problem. As far as the consequences for the customers' tastes are concerned, strangely enough there is a convergence between the critical analysis mentioned in Chapter 3 on Wal-Mart by the professor of semiotics Blonsky and that made by Hans Reischl, for many years head of the Rewe group: aesthetic smoothing and the resulting loss of the ability to make distinctions of taste. 'The taste of people who shop at Aldi becomes worse,' says Reischl.[20] 'If your aim is merely to get by, you won't starve at Aldi or Lidl. But you will not be able to enjoy the pleasures of an attractive food supply either.'[21] Cheap chic instead of polarization is the recipe. But – and this applies to both sides – those who think only in categories of expansion and slashing prices are hardly likely to achieve sustainable innovation.

Disneyfication: shaping entertainment for children today (stories instead of history)

We live in a world where people have more and more free time at their disposal. The amount of time we need to spend working in order to earn a living is falling. As leisure time is becoming more and more important and we have more and more information at our disposal, entertainment automatically becomes an increasingly dominant topic. Wherever we are and whatever we do, it is hard to imagine life without entertainment.[22] Whereas in the 1990s we said 'There's no business like show business,' today the unmistakable message is: 'There's no business without show business.' And we can add the suffix '-tainment' to all sorts of activities: infotainment, shop-o-tainment, eatertainment, confertainment, edutainment, architainment... This lends entertainment models particular significance in a rich world with increasing mobility, a rapidly ageing population and relentless technological development.

Disneyland is the original model for the modernization of children's entertainment in a media-dominated world.[23] No one saw as clearly as Disney that the dream worlds of children had to be the starting point for the creation of products and services in his theme parks: 'The most valued commodity is the human imagination.'[24] There has never been such a radical interpretation of what holidays and leisure mean to children, and so far the Disney model has been at most copied, but never significantly improved upon. Even Eurodisney, nicknamed 'cultural Chernobyl' or 'the Tragic Kingdom' by the French, has become a success over the last 10 years. The process of expansion is being continued in Asia, where further theme parks are to be built.

Disney's strength lies in the fact that, in endless variations, it tells and retells simple stories with the simplest basic structures and with a human aspect. And the environment in which the stories are set is safe and clean. As it is never a question of history, but only of stories, the politico-cultural background also becomes irrelevant. What counts is the anthropological constants, in other words such basic and universal human emotions as love, hate and the feeling of belonging. This makes the Disney stories transposable, even across cultural divides.

Today, one problem is that we don't really have any theme parks for adults. And theme parks are not really cheap. And so we have to make do with alternative forms. Structurally, of course, the entertainment-based models are similar in many ways, whether they were conceived for children or adults. Let us take a brief look at two of them.

Vegasization: shaping modern entertainment for adults (trends and the Survival of the Fittest Dream)

If you take a closer look at the range of entertainment for adults, you can say there are two models that are very similar in structure and differ only in their focus: Las Vegas and Venice. Both also offer an impressive illustration of the trends that are becoming dominant for urban conglomerations today.

Vegas is unique. A hundred years ago, the city didn't even exist. In the 1930s, it had a mere 5,000 inhabitants. In the 1970s, that figure had swelled to a good 100,000, and today the population of Las Vegas far exceeds a million (no one knows the exact figure). It is the fastest-growing city in the United States. No other city provides a better example of rapid population growth, a booming economy and a radical focus on tourism and catering to conferences, while at the same time its image has been radically transformed, from that of the seedy Sin City to a squeaky-clean US icon. And nowhere can you learn more within a short space of time, particularly about leisure and collective dream worlds.[25] And of course, there's nowhere where you can learn more about marketing and sales in their raw form, unvarnished, capitalistically uninhibited, direct. Nothing is moderate here. Vegas is essentially a theme park, at least if you look at its famous Strip, the main axis along which you find the themed hotels. In 1989, the visionary Steve Wynn built the Mirage Hotel and laid the foundation for a city that is a centre of modern entertainment situated in the middle of a desert, a city that only 10 years later was a global attraction and continues to set trends.[26] Las Vegas is the first 21st-century city.[27] It may even be the last in the series of the world's great mythical cities.

> Perhaps Las Vegas may be the last great, mythic city that Western civilization will ever create. It has birthed a slow, steady flow of cities whose very names have become symbolic of what they have offered newcomers: Baghdad, Babylon, Cairo, Athens; then Constantinople, Rome, Venice, Florence; then Paris, Vienna, Prague, Berlin, St Petersburg; now London, New York, New Orleans, Los Angeles. Like it or not, Las Vegas has joined these mythic cities.[28]

In China, manufacturers are locked in a fight for the Survival of the Cheapest. Wal-Mart has its Survival of the Fittest Logistics. And Las Vegas stands for the Survival of the Fittest Dream.[29] Quite rightly, experts speak of the Disneyfication of Las Vegas. Las Vegas has it all – it has gambling (the basis), shows, crazier and crazier themed hotels from Luxor to New York New York to Bellagio to the Venetian, more and more zany stores such as the Forum Shops in Caesar's Palace or the Aladdin, the vast array of top restaurants that appeared almost overnight, and even attempts to introduce art to attract more visitors (here again, Steve Wynn was the initiator). No other city in the USA (or indeed in the world) can boast so many top US chefs within such a small area (on the Strip) – Jean-Georges Vongerichten, Wolfgang Puck, Todd English, Emeril

Lagasse, Charlie Palmer, Nobu Matsuhisa, Julian Serrano etc – or such a collection of branches of famous restaurants (eg Olives, Spago, Nobu, Cirque, Auréole) or new stars on the restaurant scene (eg Trattoria del Lupo, Prime, Picasso).

As the first global city of the 21st century, Las Vegas also encompasses some developments that might become the models of the future. For example, since all retailers and many manufacturers have a flagship store (some more than one) in the new malls, the ambition of a brand is plain for all to see. We can observe, for example, a sort of Guccification (the successful luxury brand has several stores in the most important hotels, such as the Bellagio or Caesar's) or a Puckification (the celebrity chef has several restaurants in various price brackets, which underscore his image as the United States' top chef, for example the Wolfgang Puck Café in the MGM Grand Hotel, Spago's and Chinois in the Forum Shops, Lupo in the Mandalay Bay Hotel, Postrio in the Venetian or Cili in the Bali Hai Golf Club).

As far as costs are concerned, Vegas has the long-standing advantage of being able to subsidize its hotel rooms with the proceeds from the gambling operations that are its main source of profit. Yield management has made it possible to book a room for a Monday or a Tuesday in many hotels at much lower rates than at the weekend or in peak season. In Vegas, anyone who wishes to do so can live the Survival of the Fittest Dream at reduced prices.

As the perfect theme park for leisure activities, Vegas is also a model that sets out to meet the needs of tourism and convention guests.[30] It is a short-trip paradise run according to the criteria of efficiency and effectiveness. No normal person could stay here for long without going crazy, but then you wouldn't want to stay in an Aldi or a Wal-Mart for ever, either. The average Vegas customer spends three or four days here and, in those three or four days, he or she can have it all: spend half a day shopping, eat out at a restaurant in the early evening, go to a show later on, do some gambling in the early morning hours and do business in between times. Vegas is also the perfect expression of a time market in which the rules of the financial markets dictate the rules of the real markets.[31] Only those willing to take great risks and who are prepared to win or lose large sums as investors will be successful here.

Today, Las Vegas has a whole series of potential imitators – but these are not in the USA. Dubai is probably the copy with the greatest chance of one day achieving Las Vegas status. It has the infrastructure, the ambition and the money to do so, and the plans show that this may well happen within the foreseeable future.

Venetianization: shaping modern entertainment for adult Europeans (tradition or the soft version of Vegas – museum cities)

Venice is the model for the modernization of entertainment for adult Europeans. It may even be the original model on which all others were based, because, unlike Las Vegas, Venice was not built on trends, but on tradition.[32] Trends are for people who don't care much for tradition. Trendy people are constantly rushing around looking for the very latest must-have, the latest gimmick, the changes that keep our life dynamic. This is why trends are much more interesting for young people than for older ones. Trendy people also have no compunction about destroying something they have worked for in order to replace it with something new. Creative destruction is their game. It could also be said that people who have no weighty tradition need trends or are at least more susceptible to them. And that, of course, is why the United States is the home of trends – only the Next Big Thing is interesting enough to grab people's attention, not the achievements of the past. Americans don't want history – they want a good story, and tomorrow the story will be a different one. Culture vultures in Europe tend to interpret this as a sign of superficiality, and this is why they will prefer the 'authenticity' of Venice to the 'artificiality' of Las Vegas.

Venice is a model case of the increasingly museum-like character of many urban centres in Europe. European cities, too, are becoming centres of the leisure industry in the age of global information and entertainment. They are increasingly dependent on an influx of tourists – this is just as true of financial centres like London as of Munich or Rome. Whereas buildings were frequently torn down and replaced by new factories over the last 200 years as a result of industrialization and the technological revolution, now our urban centres are becoming museums. Buildings are no longer torn down but maintained. The message is: everything is already here! Look, this is what we once were; we are preserving the past for you! It is also the paradigm for other European cities, which, having survived wars, trade and industrialization, are now mutating to centres of leisure – just think of Glasgow, Barcelona or the Ruhr area. While Las Vegas is constantly seeking the very latest thrills and crazes for its shows and events, creating themed hotels, taking shopping to new dimensions or even becoming a world culinary centre, Venice can offer the show and spectacle of tradition.

In future, we will probably see more and more of a mixture between Vegas and Venice, because one thing is certain: competition for the mobile euro or the mobile dollar or the mobile yen will become increasingly keen. The low-price airlines could play an intermediary role here, because it is they who transport the cash-bearing, adventure-hungry tourists.

It is striking that the two cities actually have a very similar business model: they no longer produce anything; they no longer export anything; all they do is import people who perform low-paid jobs in the service sector. They base their economy on the three Cs: culture, conferences and consumption. Or, to put it in other words, on a clever blend of entertainment, education and information. They have the same personnel structures, consisting of employees whose activities in the broadest sense cater to the requirements of the postmodern leisure industry, tourism and business meetings. What they offer is cultural attractions of every kind, premium shopping, restaurants, hotels, design and memorable architecture (the so-called signature buildings). The most important and the most serious drawback in these models is that tourists drive costs up because they have higher expectations than the locals. They want to see and do as much as possible in their few days in town, and they want to do it in safety, on clean streets and with good service. The desire to please the tourists, who expect international standards, often conflicts with the wishes of the local population, who want to preserve their own local way of life. Tailoring their programme to suit the needs of an international or national clientele with a large number of private security personnel, jazzed-up shopping boulevards and overpriced services may boost the quality of life for the tourists, but at the same time it detracts from that of the people who live there. This is one of the sources of tension we find in many large European towns and cities that are in the process of becoming museums.

Just how influential the Italian cities are as models can also be seen in the fact that there are many imitation Venices. In Belek in southern Turkey, there is a large leisure hotel called the Venice – the symbol of the Campanile is its trademark. And one of Las Vegas's most attractive hotels is the Venetian, a faithful replica of the Campanile and many other Venetian attractions, right down to the Canale Grande, a shopping boulevard with a real canal, gondoliers and opera. We can learn something from this: in an upwardly mobile world where information is communicated at an increasing pace, destinations are also becoming transposable. They need a physical location, but the models take on a symbolic character and become icons, and, the stronger this image is, the more it is cloned and reproduced all over the planet. And because Venice is such a strong model, it exists in many different forms in the global image economy. This is an advantage in a world in which people can and do visit destinations all over the globe and in which entertainment, museum cities, trends and tradition converge.

Why are these models so rational and so successful?[33]

In the end, it is a combination of principles and criteria that makes these models so strong.

Increased efficiency and simplicity

Efficiency means achieving a predefined aim with optimum – economic – use of means. The most efficient way to go from 'hungry' to 'full' is at McDonald's. At Wal-Mart, I have the guarantee that the distribution of any product I buy, from the loading bay at Procter & Gamble to the boot of my car, is organized with unparalleled efficiency and to industrial standards. At Aldi, I know they don't engage in any extraneous activities that would make goods more expensive. At easyJet, I know that I can make reservations quickly and easily online. I know that I can get from my airport of departure to my final destination more efficiently than with many national carriers, because secondary airports have lower charges. And Las Vegas shows me how I can get the maximum holiday experience in a minimum of time.

- If we take the logic of efficiency further, we will see that efficiency and simplicity are an ideal combination. Aldi shows us that by not increasing its range of goods it can avoid squandering its energies. If it stocked more articles, it would have more suppliers and would require a greater coordination effort, which would quickly find its expression in disproportionally high prices. From Ryanair or Southwest, we can learn that it is best to restrict oneself to one type of plane and that handling should be reduced to a minimum so that planes do not spend too much unnecessary and unproductive time on the ground. For McDonald's, providing a more efficient service for the customer will mean growth in the Drive Thru business, where customers do not have to get out of their vehicle and stand in a queue, but can place their order and get their meal in the comfort of their car. This means additional security and control for the customer. And if you keep your operation efficient and simple, you can implement new ideas more quickly. The fast food chain opened its first Drive Thru in Oklahoma City in 1975 and, within the space of just four years, almost half the McDonald's restaurants in the United States had done likewise. Simplicity means not only a limited number of articles, but also simple products. One of the greatest revolutions in our eating habits over the last hundred years was the 'demilitarization' of eating: I need neither knife nor fork to eat my meal, and a handy sign shows me a comfortable range of products I can choose from.[34]

- For a provider of goods and services, the best way to boost your efficiency in a dynamic and complex world is to begin outsourcing. Stelios Haji-Ioannou realized that it was possible to delegate tasks to the customer, step by step, under the motto 'outsourcing to the customer'. In particular, successful business models in the services sector, for example airlines, work according to the principle of providing services with high fixed costs and price elasticity – this means that customers are typically inclined to buy more as soon as prices fall – and making communication easier, for example online reservation. Then give your customers a clever, but limited, selection of possibilities, such as that offered by the easyDorm hotel concept, where customers book a room online, make up their own beds, clear up after themselves as required etc. And the more guests are prepared to do for themselves, the lower the final price will be. Obviously, the goal here is for customers to do everything for themselves, as this is the most attractive option for the provider. It enables the hotel to boost its efficiency, simplifies handling and makes for more predictable results.

- For many models, the core area where efficiency can be increased is probably logistical competence: at Wal-Mart, for example, which sees its role as that of a distributor for its customers, or at Aldi, where shelf arrangements and stacking on pallets simplify logistics. And Zara and Hennes & Mauritz (H&M) both have a faster turnaround of articles than any other comparable retailer.

- Another point to consider here is cutting out the intermediary. A strong retailer will achieve the maximum possible degree of independence and seek direct access to the final consumer and to manufacturers, thus sidestepping any intermediaries earning their cut. They would only make things more complicated and thus more cost-intensive.

- However, boosting efficiency also means simplification via lower personnel costs. The low-price airlines are the experts here. In 2003, Ryanair flew around 24 million passengers with only 2,000 employees, while Lufthansa (O'Leary refers to it as 'Lufty') had 48 million passengers, double the figure, but a workforce of 30,000. Wal-Mart employs many skilled workers laid off from other industries on conditions applicable to unskilled labour. These business models are often a thorn in the side of the unions, and the businesses usually want no truck with organized labour – see Ryanair or Wal-Mart. Wal-Mart pays its staff in the USA an average hourly wage of $8.50, as compared with $13 paid by supermarkets whose staff are union members.[35]

- Ultimately, boosting efficiency means optimization of exist-ing goods and services through attention to detail. Aim to do what you already do better, not to find new products. And that is what the low-price airlines do so perfectly. Yield management allows them to fine-tune their capacity utiliza-tion and control their operations in real time.

Calculability and no frills

To ensure calculability, all the critical factors need to be quantifi-able from the outset – the size of portions, the time allowed to make a Big Mac or Whopper, costs for infrastructure, personnel deployment etc. The basic principle here is 'bigger is better'. This is why development in the fast food trade has essentially led to bigger portions and the resulting price scales.

- The margins for soft drinks or french fries, for example, are incredible, often several hundred per cent. The more the customer consumes, the cheaper it is. Super Size fries mean 20 per cent more per portion, and the Double Burger is of course followed by the Triple Burger. The effort required to provide the larger portion is minimal. In widely varying industries, 'bigger is better' has led to the 'stretching' of products. 'Americans tend to stretch everything,' says Chris Muller.[36]
- Within a company, calculability largely means a no-nonsense culture and no-frills operations. The corollary to 'bigger is better' is 'less is more'. Anything that is not absolutely essen-tial on the input side goes overboard. Aldi is the consum-mate example here.[37] 'The only thing that interests us in our calculation is how cheaply we can sell a product.'[38] Nothing else counts.

While it can safely be assumed that many easyJet employ-ees still enjoy their jobs to some extent, the company culture at Aldi is very hard-working, as it is too at Wal-Mart, but under different conditions. Ryanair has a typical 'Work them hard' culture. Their pilots fly twice as many miles a month as those at British Airways, close to the legal limit, but their salaries are also significantly higher than those paid by the national carrier and the career chances are good.

- Paradoxically, calculability also means that skilful insourcing is necessary. Advertising is not handled by agencies; the do-it-yourself approach is the rule of the day. Do it yourself and you understand it better. Let others do it and you lose control. Your independence and identity suffer. It is a well-known fact that Aldi spends much less on advertising than other retailers, namely 0.3 per cent of its turnover.[39] Its rivals easily spend twice or three times as much. Zara does not advertise at all, relying instead on word of mouth.

- In this way, many low-price operators surround themselves with the aura of skilled amateurs. They are not prepared to spend money on the (pseudo-) professional services of consultants or agencies. Thus, we can also say that, in the case of many successful business models, calculability leads to a general mistrust of consultants. Stelios of easyJet was quick to realize that, instead of improving the results of his Easy-Internet cafés, a consultancy agreement with HP (Hewlett-Packard) could lead to skyrocketing support costs per PC.[40] And so the company now works with standard equipment and normal off-the-shelf technology. This has not only drastically reduced costs but has also had no negative effects whatsoever for customers.

- The most obvious point is perhaps that calculability means focusing clearly on one thing – the price. No meals, no refund policy, no assigned places. Only by keeping your eyes fixed rigidly on your limited range of services can you retain your grip on costs. Stelios boasts that, by adhering to his no-frills philosophy and not providing food and drinks on board as a standard service, he was the first to give his flight attendants the chance to earn tips on a regular basis by selling snacks and refreshments.

Predictability and no unpleasant surprises

'Satisfaction guaranteed' puts this form of rationalization in a nutshell. There are no unforeseens. I know in advance what I'm getting and what I will be experiencing. A Whopper tastes the same all over the world. The authority in this sector is probably Disneyland. Efficiency and calculability are preconditions here, too, but no one combines this so perfectly with the predictability of the experience as Disney.

- If you want to achieve predictability, a forced ritualization of processes is important, in particular where interaction with customers is concerned. As efficiency demands that this interaction be very brief, where necessary it will follow a predefined script. Thus, the interaction will inevitably become theatricalized and emotionalized. 'May I help you?' becomes 'Melpyou?', and the answer follows in the same breath: 'Fries?'[41] And it's even more apparent in the Drive Thru. The employee's 'Melpyou?' is uttered so quickly it almost disappears altogether. The aim is to save one- or two-tenths of a second – after all, every three seconds saved between taking an order and handing over the goods at the Drive Thru boosts turnover on average by 1 per cent.

- Predictability reflects another trend in our entertainment culture: consumers who spend 100 euros on a ticket for a football match or a concert want guaranteed success. They do not want to be bored. This is a particular priority in the case of (pure) entertainment models. If no goals are scored, the organizers have to plan in as many other entertainment elements as to ensure the spectators go home happy even if the game is bad. This is why more and more new stadiums are built with roofed-over seating. In Las Vegas, everything that forms part of the Vegas experience takes place under a roof: from the shows to shopping facilities, gaming halls and car parks. You can't afford disappointments in an age in which a strong 'emotional return' within a brief space of time is increasingly important compared with other factors.

- So, essentially, predictability means don't disappoint the punters. The advantage of the models described here is that I always know in advance what level of disappointment awaits me. O'Leary of Ryanair freely admits that, for such low prices, the customer can no longer expect his staff to smile and be friendly all the time. All I can expect is to be flown punctually and comfortably from A to B. The price does not cover any additional expectations. This point cannot be made emphatically enough in view of the fact that most companies, bound up in the desire to increase so-called customer orientation and provide added value, introduced additional services to their range, which simply increased the price. No one thought to ask whether this was really what the customer wanted. This was one of the core problems faced by the national carriers. For the airlines – at least on short-haul flights – customer satisfaction means primarily that customers get a good deal and reach their destination within the given time.

Control and repetition

Modern technology allows us to eradicate possible sources of error. From the moment we enter a store to the moment we leave it, every step is carefully controlled.

In actual fact, machines could take over all the work – and so the employees, like machines, have a limited and clearly defined task: the grill people, the fry people, the dressers. And so the increasing trend towards control over operations means that routinization is increased to the max and work steps are made as repetitive as possible. The system runs so perfectly that operations are kept under total control. This entails, for example, making sure – from the customer and the employee side – that customers spend only a controlled amount of time in the store or restaurant. While in Europe it would still be considered impolite to slap the bill on the table while customers are chewing the last mouthfuls of their meal, it has become routine to do so in the USA, or at least to ask the customer to vacate the table and go to the bar, thus vacating the table for the next guest.[42] This is another consequence of the increasingly perfect implementation of yield management.

The four criteria and principles for success of business models summarized here will become more adaptable and increase in their significance for the future if we work from the premise that deregularization, liberalization and privatization are going to progress over the coming months and years. But then, modernization always is paradoxical.

Rationalization models have their limits – and when they exceed them they become irrational

While on the one hand there are clearly benefits to be gained for all participants in this system – efficiency, calculability, predictability and control mean growth and prosperity – there is a certain point beyond which benefits increasingly become disadvantages. Rational intentions have irrational consequences; models of rationalization become irrational.

While on the positive side availability, reachability, comparability, security and familiarity have increased, on the negative side there are unplanned side-effects. Queues are getting longer. The time I gain in eating I lose standing in a queue. The time I actually spend on the rides on an average one-day visit to Disneyland is minimal. I spend most of my time queuing, easily an hour per attraction, for less than two minutes of fun, and then I can get in the next queue for the next ride. An example puts this into perspective. A customer has calculated that one hour of pure ride-time could easily cost US $261.[43] Wal-Mart helps its customers save over US $100 billion a year, but at the same time its employees' hourly wage is steadily sinking. Another factor that is often overlooked is that such low-wage jobs have extremely high turnover rates – while turnovers of up to 100 per cent or 150 per cent are possible in the retail trade, the rate can be as high as 300 per cent in the fast food industry. That means that the average employee stays with a company for only four months – as soon as employees are offered more money else-where, they will leave. The US economy provides an impressive and unparalleled example of this: whenever economic activity picks up, employees' attitudes become less customer-oriented. As their wages fall, they are constantly on the lookout for ways to improve their income, and they will quit as soon as they can get 0.3 dollar more an hour elsewhere. Job hopping is on the increase. People start a job only to switch to another firm at the drop of a hat. On the other hand, if the economy is slow employ-ees are more customer-oriented and stay in one job longer. In the catering sector, there is the added problem caused by the tipping culture. The problem has become worse in the years of recession following the terrorist attacks of 11 September 2001. As a customer, I am expected to add a 15 per cent tip to the amount on the bill, even if the service was bad. (And if I tip less, I can probably expect to be pressurized to give a good reason for it or to be treated in a very unfriendly manner. In this sector, particularly in the USA, making the reward dependent on the quality of the service is an unknown concept.)

How does this mechanism work? By turning the screw and accelerating the spiral. Because jobs are reduced to monotonous and routine steps, they are low-paid. Because they are low-paid, people change jobs more often. To make jobs even simpler and thus make it easier to find and train new personnel, they become more monotonous. Thus, control is increased and predictability means efficiency. And so it goes on.

Museumized urban centres practise outsourcing of all visible problems: they are relegated to the suburbs. Our leisure cities must appear clean, safe and attractive. Paris is a wonderful example of this. Paris is Venice, is Disney, is Las Vegas. So far, the French capital has managed to outsource all its problems, which are mainly of a social or environmental nature. In the city centre, you have the museums, now transformed into leisure temples. On the edge of this area, like a belt, there is a sort of fortified wall of the really big shopping centres such as Carrefour and Auchan together with the Ibis and Formule 1 hotels. Beyond that you have the unwelcoming *banlieues*. And a little further out, there are the leisure (shopping) parks Eurodisney, Val d'Europe (Auchan again) and Carré Sénart (Carrefour again).

What conclusion can we draw from this? It is easy to transfer these rationalization models with their criteria and their principles of success to other sectors – they will work there, too, though perhaps less perfectly – for example, to the health-care sector (eg the attempts to optimize health plans), to the universities and education in general (the increasing importance accorded to rankings and to benchmarking educational institutions, and the importance placed on the number of publications to date when evaluating lecturers – 'publish or perish'), to sport (for example football, where state-of-the-art technology, scanners and cameras make it possible to capture every quantifiable aspect, make a statistic of it and use it to evaluate the game) and even to politics (where, thanks to instant polling, we can get a real-time assessment of the political mood at any given moment). At best in, for example, football or politics, we get added entertainment value, but the information value decreases. There tend to be more losers than winners.

However, this is only logical. The factors that bring about the success of these rationalization models also mean that everyone takes the shortest route. And that leads to the following paradox: 'Only by taking a roundabout route can we exist. If everyone took the shortest route, only one would reach the finishing line.'[44] In our culture, we tend to see only the shortest route as sensible.

Notes

[1] McDonald's has been even more thoroughly studied than Disney. Works on the subject include John F Love (1986) *McDonald's: Behind the arches*, Bantam Books, New York. For a very good overview of and insight into McDonald's in East Asia, see the excellent collected edition edited by James L Watson (1997) *Golden Arches East: McDonald's in East Asia*, Stanford University Press, Stanford, CA.

[2] George Ritzer (1996) *The McDonaldization of Society: An investigation into the changing character of contemporary social life*, rev edn, Pine Forge Press, Thousand Oaks, CA; and by the same author (1998) *The McDonaldization Thesis: Explorations and extensions*, Sage, London.

[3] Ritzer, *The McDonaldization Thesis*, p 33.

[4] The business press, from the *Wall Street Journal* to the *Financial Times*, as well as *USA Today*, regularly feature articles on the situation in the fast food trade, in particular, of course, McDonald's. They all affirm that it is impossible to create the classic fast food business anew. For obvious reasons, one should be wary of this statement.

[5] Quoted in Shirley Leung (2003) 'A glutted US market makes fast-food chains hungry for fresh sites', *Wall Street Journal Europe*, 2 October, pp A1, A6.

[6] Statement made by the CEO of Ikea Foodservice, Jan Kjellman, at the 3rd European Foodservice Summit, 24–25 September 2002, Zurich.

[7] See Robert Slater (2003) *The Wal-Mart Decade: How a new generation of leaders turned Sam Walton's legacy into the world's number one company*, Portfolio.

[8] Stelios Haji-Ioannou, for example, freely admits that Southwest was the role model for the development of easyJet (in an interview given to me at the 4th European Foodservice Summit, 25–26 September 2003, Zurich).

[9] On the subject of the low-price airline revolution, see Simon Calder and Freddie Laker (2002) *No Frills: The truth behind the low cost revolution in the skies*, Virgin Publishing, London; and, particularly on the subject of Southwest, Lamar Muse (2003) *Southwest Passage: The inside*

story of Southwest Airline's formative years, Eakin Publications, Austin, TX; and Judy Hoffer Gittell (2003) *The Southwest Airlines Way: Using the power of relationships to achieve high performance*, McGraw-Hill, New York.

[10] Quoted in the *Financial Times*, 21/22 June 2003, p W2.

[11] Howard Schultz, the founder and strategic head of the coffee chain, described its history and his motivation in book form; see Howard Schultz (1999) *Pour Your Heart into It: How Starbucks built a company one cup at a time*, Hyperion Press, New York.

[12] Of course, the premium brands also profited from this, from Nespresso to Illy, which is a good illustration of how strongly segmented and differentiated a coffee market can be.

[13] For example, see the websites ihatestarbucks.com or starbucked.com. In the meantime, whole US communities have become anti-Starbucks communities, for example Excelsior in Minnesota; see Debbie Howlett, 'Minnesota small town just says no to "Starbucks Nation"', *USA Today*, 2 October 2003, p 5A.

[14] See 'Wal-Mart expands RFID mandate', *RFID Journal*, 18 August 2003.

[15] According to Dieter Brandes, 53rd International Trade Congress of the GDI, 15–16 September 2003.

[16] For a wealth of similar, partly curious and humorous findings, see Hannes Hintermaier (1998) *Die ALDI-Welt: Nachforschungen im Reich der Diskount-Milliardäre*, Karl Blessing Verlag, Munich.

[17] See www.koever.com/aldi/forum, 17 June 2003.

[18] Website as above.

[19] *Rheinischer Merkur*, 4/1998.

[20] See the interview with Hans Reischl, 'Wer bei Aldi kauft, verarmt im Geschmack', *FAZ-Sonntagszeitung*, 13 April 2003, No. 15, p 35.

[21] In the article cited above.

[22] See Michael J Wolf (1999) *The Entertainment Economy: How mega-media forces are transforming our lives*, Random House, New York. Although the main focus of the book is on the media, it does highlight many interesting aspects of our entertainment landscape.

[23] Hardly any phenomenon has been so thoroughly studied in all its aspects, from the commercial to the religious or social, as Disney and Disneyland. See also David Lyon (2000) *Jesus in Disneyland: Religion in postmodern times*, Blackwell, Malden; Andrew Lainsbury (2000) *Once upon an American Dream: The story of Euro Disneyland*, University of Kansas Press, Kansas.

[24] Michael J Wolf, *The Entertainment Economy*, p 296.

[25] On the subject of dream worlds, see Rolf Jensen's wonderful book (1999) *The Dream Society: How the coming shift from information to imagination will transform your business*, McGraw-Hill, New York.

[26] Over the last few years, a lot of research has been done into Las Vegas. See, for example, Pete Earley (2000) *Super Casino: Inside the 'new' Las Vegas*, Bantam, New York; or Andrés Martinez (1999) *24/7: Living it up and doubling down in the new Las Vegas*, Villard, New York.

[27] See David Bosshart (2000) 'Trendlabor: Lernen von der ersten globalen Stadt des 21. Jahrhunderts', *NZZ Folio*, August, pp 62–63.

[28] See James B Twitchell (2002) *Living It Up: Our love affair with luxury*, Columbia University Press, New York, p 219, also see pp 215–68.

[29] The expression 'Survival of the Fittest Dream' was coined by Twitchell, in the work cited above, p 219.

[30] See Mark Gottdiener, Claudia C Collins and David R Dickens (1999) *Las Vegas: The social production of an all-American city*, Blackwell, Malden. The book gives a wonderful overview of all the problems and opportunities of a themed city like Las Vegas and contains interesting perspectives for the future.

[31] See Chapter 5.

[32] Many works by Hermann Lübbe deal with the subject of trend and tradition, though from a different perspective, for example *Zwischen Trend und Tradition: Überfordert uns die Gegenwart?*, Interfrom, Zurich, 1981, and *Im Zug der Zeit: Verkürzter Aufenthalt in der Gegenwart*, Springer, Berlin, 1994.

[33] On this subject, see George Ritzer's basic study (1996) *The McDonaldization of Society*, rev edn, Pine Forge Press, Thousand Oaks, CA.

[34] It is a well-known phenomenon that the majority of fast food customers order first and look at the sign second. This has something to do with the familiarity of the product – you just take a look to check.

[35] See Steven Greenhouse (2003) 'Wal-Mart driving workers and supermarkets crazy', *New York Times*, 19 October, p 3.

[36] Chris Muller is the incumbent of a unique chair for 'Multiunit Restaurant Management' in the USA, and therefore the expert on gastronomy chains. He lectures at the University of Central Florida, Orlando.

[37] For a very good, authentic description, see Dieter Brandes's (1998) book *Konsequent einfach: Die ALDI-Erfolgsstory*, Campus, Frankfurt.

[38] In the work cited above, p 19.

[39] According to Dieter Brandes, in the work cited above, p 220.

[40] See David Kirkpatrick (2003) 'How to erase the middleman in one easy lesson', *Fortune*, 17 March, p 76.

[41] On this point, see Jim Taylor and Watts Wacker (1997) *The 500-Year Delta: What happens after what comes next?*, Harper, New York, p 82.

[42] Paradoxically, it is the luxury restaurants that are most advanced here. Charles Palmer's famous restaurant, Auréole, in Las Vegas has 16 hidden cameras in the restaurant area. They send digital information into the kitchen. 'You can zoom in and see if the fork's on the plate,' says Palmer. This monitoring system is claimed to increase efficiency by 30 per cent and help achieve a faster turnaround of guests. Digital video systems are getting cheaper, and are now available for as little as US $10,000.

[43] Derived from Ritzer, *The McDonaldization of Society*, p 125.

[44] From Hans Blomberg (1988) *Die Sorge geht über den Fluss*, Suhrkamp, Frankfurt, p 137.

5 Faster, better, cheaper

Intensified time markets drive the
Age of Cheap

I'm religious about the way I manage my time.[1]
Steve Ballmer, CEO Microsoft

The history of economic progress consists of charging a fee
for what once was free.[2]
Gilmore and Pine, *The Experience Economy*

If efficiency boosting and simplicity, calculability and no frills, predictability and the ruling out of unpleasant surprises, control and repetition are ultimately among the central values that are essential for a modernization of our economy and society in the Age of Cheap, this means that, in the end, our markets become time markets. Time has always been an important factor, but now time has really become our most important resource in the fight for market shares.

Time as an economic factor

Over the last few years and decades, traditional business models have gradually shown us that it is not enough to focus one's attention only on money and price. From industry through trade to the service providers, we have developed just-in-time concepts, speed management, time management, ECR (efficient consumer response), CM (category management), CRM (customer relationship management), yield management and more and more sophisticated dynamic pricing concepts. Economic progress consists in charging for something that was once free as soon as there is interest in a particular service that at first sight does not seem to have an obvious monetary value.

Time is an even more abstract resource than money and thus potentially more valuable. So while we have long since integrated the concept of time into sectors of the economy ranging from industry to services, on the all-important consumer side of our business transactions the resource money or the price remains in the foreground. Today, time is usually a hidden cost that is not taken into consideration when calculating effort involved on the customer side.

As we have no reason to assume that it is possible to remain untouched by economization in all areas of life, the indication is that things will continue to move faster and faster.[3] On global markets where information is more and more easy to obtain, the chances of exploiting the advantage of time to earn money over a longer period of time are dwindling, and the chances of your product immediately being imitated are increasingly high. This applies to everything from consumer products to pharmaceuticals. And so the providers of goods and services have to find a way to earn money with their existing time bonus. On the customer side, the perception of time has also changed dramatically. In a world where we are confronted with an abundance of offers and less and less time at our disposal, we place increased value on anything that helps us to save time. In a world of deregulation and globalization, the first product to appear on the market and attract attention to itself is the most valuable. This is a logical consequence of the development of the Western nations. The richer we become, the more important the time factor is. The richer we become, the more we long to have more time for the important things in life. As far as economic activity is concerned, this means that anyone who fails to understand the time factor will become its victim.[4] And so the more we realize that time is the key resource at our disposal and that it is a non-renewable resource, the more value will be accorded to it economically and the more customers will be charged for it in the form of price or margin factors. The whole convenience food sector with its pre-cooked meals is based on this, as are many areas of the wellness sector with its short cuts in body care: stay younger faster. And so it is not enough simply to rationalize processes and work sequences so that they save time. We must learn to appreciate the customer's hidden costs. For this reason, we believe that the dominant topic in coming years will be saving time, especially in connection with the observation of and research into the customer side. This means that the following questions are both relevant and of economic interest:

- How can the time factor be integrated into products and services?
- How far are customers prepared to pay for time saved?
- What time innovations will there be in future?
- Why is it that the low-price operators have the edge here too?
- And also: where is time not a competitive benefit, or where is the resource of time not available in unlimited supply?

The logic of increase (Logic No. 1)

First, let us examine the question as to what the further development of the time factor will be. We can distinguish two fundamental paths of logic here (see Figure 5.1).

Logic 1: The logic of increase

We function according to the motto 'faster, better, cheaper'. This is the bulldozer so perfectly embodied by Wal-Mart. This is the mainstream of business today. It is about trying to be successful by following the classic rules of economies of scale. And a company that does so successfully can then try to implement 'bigger, more global, more standardized'. Thus our economies follow a simple logic of increase: more of the same. What our managers are taught in their management seminars can be summarized simply as 'more and more, more is more'. And the further we progress, the more more is more. The unusual circumstances and the irrational fervour of the scandal-laden years 1998–2002 provided a very clear example of where this logic will lead if no corrective measures are taken. Today we can see this logic still at work, only now there is a little less of the irrational enthusiasm – and, for example, greater publicity and the immediate uncovering of scandals.

Logic of increase	Logic of differentiation
More and more, more is more	Less is more
Synchronization, seamless, fault-free	Asymmetries of speed
Faster, cheaper, better	Only two of these
If everyone takes the shortest route, only one will reach the finishing line	Less but best – find intelligent alternative paths

GDI©

Figure 5.1 Two logics: increase or differentiation

The 'more is more' logic is pursued to the bitter end. Look, for example, at the retail trade in Germany, Switzerland or Britain. There are plans for even more expansion, although these countries have long had too many shops and many consumers have already exhausted their financial reserves, spent too much and overfilled their homes.[5] Everyone wants growth. 'Survival of the Fittest' continues to be the watchword: either 'Survival of the Fittest Logistics' (Wal-Mart, Aldi) or 'Survival of the Fittest Dreams' (Vegas, Venice).

However, what is perhaps most surprising is that we fail to learn with experience. The logic 'faster, better, cheaper' and 'bigger, more global, more standardized' continues to dominate, seemingly unquestioned by anyone. The individual sectors doggedly pursue their logic and while away their time with so-called 'trivial learning' – they do what they can, just more energetically. The more companies engage in benchmarking, the more the results will be even more similar. And when that happens, we become a civilization of superfluity and the over-abundance continues. Let us summarize:

1. There is too much of everything.
2. Even those who can afford not to do it watch their money.
3. Those who have little money want something good too.
4. And everyone wants pleasure without pain.

The retail trade reacts with larger and larger stores. More of the same. In all the rich nations, the size of stores is increasing. In the USA, there is a total sales area of 777,350,000 square metres, in Europe 180,600,000 square metres. Calculated per capita, the USA has 2.9 square metres of sales area per inhabitant, Britain 0.9 square metre, France 0.8 square metre and Switzerland and Sweden 0.7 square metre. Moreover, it is interesting that today's answer to expansion in area is the same everywhere – additional shopping space outside the classic sales areas. The airport is a shopping mall (Heathrow is a prime example). The station is a shopping centre. Football stadiums are becoming shopping centres (see the new Joggeli in Basle). Universities have become shopping centres (see the Harvard Business School and the big business schools in general, which are very commercialized). Even the Church has become a shopping centre (in the Vatican, you can buy a CD with the Pope as a rapper). Yet this is a lethal game. Sales areas are increasing, but at the same time area productivity is dwindling. This situation is unacceptable in the long term. Sooner or later we will be unable to handle the complexity.

There are other barriers impeding this linear expansion. Private consumption only increases in very specific sectors, and the low-cost operators are on the ascendant everywhere. Overcapacity is rife. The big retail groups are deeper and deeper in debt. The most effective and most efficient tool is always price, so costs have to be cut further. The price war in the distribution channels continues. This is how the game goes. Customers are more selective and price becomes more important. Products become more and more interchangeable. Manufacturers' brands gain ground on retailers' own brands because they have larger margins. Customer loyalty decreases still further. Shopping becomes boring and is seen as a chore. Customers buy less; the markets shrink...

More is more. In future, it will only be possible with consistent effort to save time. All industries have realized this and have either consciously or unconsciously picked up and implemented this in their conceptualization. On the manufacturing side, 'just-in-time' emerged as a concept over 20 years ago. Time management or speed management was seen as a means to accelerate processes with support from IT. Various methods were developed. While money can be manipulated and steered with the help of know-how, it is an undisputed fact that time is a non-renewable resource and thus the most precious commodity when competing on the markets.[6] And what is true of industry is also true of trade.

Developments in trade over the last 15 years, for example ECR (efficient consumer response) or CM (category management), only serve one purpose in the end: to accelerate processes – the official argument is always customer orientation, but that is no more than a euphemism. And – it cannot be stressed too often – there is no more perfect model in this respect than Wal-Mart.

Real markets mimic financial markets

It is logical that global high-tech developments and the implementation of IT infrastructures accommodate this faster-better-cheaper world. We install more and more servers and lightweight computers and have smaller and smaller monitors that are easier and easier to transport. The exchange of information is becoming child's play. Or, to put it another way, it is becoming easier and easier and cheaper and cheaper for us to exchange more and more information more and more rapidly.

There is more and more information available. And access to it is easier than ever before. The price for good information is falling. Of course, modern information and communications technology is a contributing factor: mobile phones, e-mail, voice-mail etc. But this has a surprising effect: it tends to lend real markets some of the characteristics of financial markets. Real markets mimic financial markets.[7] So whatever we learn from the financial markets and their mechanisms (for example on the stock market) will apply increasingly to industry, consumer goods and services of all kinds. There are three central characteristics:

- *Accessibility.* Access is increasingly easy and the conditions are improving. The world of information is in the process of becoming 'googled'. Potentially, this strengthens every link in the added value chain, but above all the hitherto weakest link in it, the final consumer. If you have a bone to pick with enterprises or state institutions today, you have more and better information at your fingertips than ever before. It is of course true that easier access also means there is a greater proportion of nonsense out there. The internet really is like a vast toilet wall. But it is also true that, more than any comparable communication channel in the past, the internet empowers individuals in a new way, giving them access to better information, making it easier for them to hold their own against anyone they like and at prices that could not be more humane. However, accessibility under very simple conditions is one of the most important driving forces behind the Age of Cheap.

- *Transparency* is there for the taking. It is becoming more and more difficult to hide anything – don't even try, you're bound to be found out. Even private companies that are not stock exchange listed are facing increasing pressure to make their processes and results public. The ongoing crisis in the auditing institutions or in consulting in general will continue to favour and accelerate this development. In other words, discretion, one of the core competences in the financial services sector, is an increasingly rare commodity and becoming much harder to get. Even rerouting an e-mail can lead to claims for damages amounting to hundreds of millions, as we have seen several times over the past few years.

- *Real-time data.* We are on our way to becoming a world of information in which constant communicative feedback in real time is expected of us. At the same time, perhaps the most exciting and decisive factor is the convergence with and imitation of the financial markets. The tendency is to eliminate delay, and delay was the basis of the old hierarchical organization forms and asymmetrical relationships. We can experience change live and in real time, in the same way as the stock market prices rise and fall in real time. Immediate orientation is becoming the rule. Our children are a good example. Growing up in a world of mobile phones and SMS, they live in infinite loops. They are always tuned in, always just one node in an endless network of users who react immediately to every impulse. And so children just can't wait. They have been trained – and Wal-Mart had a hand in this – to expect immediate gratification of their wishes. Waiting is something we are less and less able to tolerate. This is particularly true when you are surfing the internet. If you don't get to the website you want immediately, you click away.

However, this is only the more harmless side of the story. Nowadays, we can also watch in real time as historic events take place. We saw this on 11 September 2001. We watched live on TV as terrorist attacks brought the Twin Towers crashing to the ground. Just a few years before, news like this would only have been released after a process of political filtering and furnished with appropriate government statements. Today, it hits the – mostly unprepared – viewers all over the world straight in the face. And their reaction is then analogous to the mechanisms of the stock markets: more emotional, above all more spontaneous, more aggressive, more informal. They give their emotions free rein, and this in turn feeds the media, enabling them to continue plying their trade.

Let us consider another example as a further illustration of this change. What would have happened with SARS (Severe Acute Respiratory Syndrome) 10 or 20 years ago? Not long ago, in a world without a real-time economy, a phenomenon like SARS would probably still have been a subject for debate among special-ists in a university hospital months after the first case appeared. Perhaps there would have been a scientific congress on it. We would probably never have heard anything about it in the media – for example on TV. Medical journals might have written about it and, much later, their articles might have been mentioned in a few of the daily newspapers. For political reasons alone, such news would have been handled with more discretion. Today, a phenom-enon like SARS has more the character of an informed rumour. Before we know what it's really about – what causes it, how to deal with it, how dangerous it really is – the unrelenting media hype has already begun. We hear and read about it in all the media; we cannot escape it. The well-meaning will object that there is a duty to inform and will talk about the necessity of not withholding information. This may be politically correct and correspond to our idea of democracy today, even if most people don't know what has hit them, but the consequences of making such information public immediately and in unfiltered form are at least as controversial. Not only does a diffuse sense of panic break out among the popu-lation, but there are also immediate and dire consequences for the economy, for example in the tourist trade. Flight reservations and holiday bookings were cancelled and business trips to the region where SARS was discovered were interrupted or postponed indef-initely. Of course, for companies that were in difficulties at the time, SARS was a welcome excuse to explain away their failure and forbid their employees to fly to these areas.

We can see for ourselves in everyday business life how a lasting change in attitude is taking place. A real-time economy alters people's expectations. If we find typing errors in a business letter, we conclude that the company that sent it is slightly dubious. If we find a typing error in a fax, we may think the same, but are proba-bly inclined to be more generous in our judgement. After all, initially we expect the letter to be correct, as otherwise we would be forced to doubt the seriousness of its content. Yet no one is bothered by a sloppily written e-mail full of mistakes arriving on their laptop. It's becoming the norm. Why? Because here, we are working with another medium, a medium in which the only thing that matters is an immediate answer so that we can quickly get on with things without wasting time. Just like the mechanisms of the stock exchange, e-mails or mobile phones with SMS evoke real-time expectations and thus automatically a more emotional context – aggressive, informal, less discreet.

Or take another example we are all more than familiar with today: instant polling in politics. We are expected to keep up to date on the candidates' prospects in coming elections. So polls are conducted in real time and it is proudly announced that on Friday 17 November 47.3 per cent of those asked would have voted for a particular candidate, whereas one week earlier that figure was 49.1 per cent. Above all else, such polls teach us one thing: politics has become like show business, a game in which the aim is to tug on the heartstrings of the masses. The only insight to be gained is of a purely emotional nature and it has entertainment value only. We learn nothing of substance. The need to be able just to get on with things takes precedence over substance. We communicate solely so that we can keep on communicating. We gather information in order to stay in the loop.

Economically, of course, the real-time economy and the transfer of stock market mechanisms to real markets has its own hard logic. Whereas profits were hitherto dependent on being able to utilize the advantage of time, in a real-time economy profits dip towards zero. Because there is less regulation by the state and because competition allows access to better information, the old advantages to be gained from withholding information strategically – secrecy, monopolization – can no longer be sustained.[8] This is the problem faced increasingly by bureaucracies of any kind. Large-scale organizations only function effectively when they can work with temporal delays. The larger an organization is, the more it needs this time factor from the point of view of the transaction costs involved alone.[9] Where these advantages shrink in the face of keener competition, the organization is forced to reorganize itself – by means of flexible networks, outsourcing models or focusing on core competences.

Theoretically, we can say that the better the market mechanism works, the quicker the competition reacts and imitates, the more the development of advantages of time will represent an asymptotic curve on a graph. For the players on the market, this means that, in an economy with a focus on real time, nothing counts as much as the moment in which a particular service is expected to be rendered – the price is then the result of factors calculated on a real-time basis. These preconditions also apply to politics and, in the present day, especially to terrorism.

Let us take this through to its logical conclusion. We can say that Bin Laden is stronger than George W Bush. Terrorists have the advantage of being able to operate without a large-scale bureaucratic organization and of being able to identify the obvious weak points of such an organization and use that knowledge to further their own aims. If you don't have the money to buy high-tech and cruise missiles, just use two passenger planes. In a connected world, that is just as effective and efficient and above all much cheaper. An analysis of acts of terrorism[10] shows us that we have to learn to understand violence, too, in terms of time saving. We live in an age of competitive violence, and those engaging in war or warlike activities today, such as postmodern terrorists, will first carry out a time analysis to find out the most effective, most efficient and cheapest method of achieving their aims. Discount wars or cheap violence will, unfortunately, probably always have a future. We will experience not only more discount wars in trade but also more civil-warlike situations.

In many ways, the real markets mimic the financial markets: prices and values float, and customer relations are no longer tested by means of the advantage of time and superior knowledge. The most important points are summarized in Figure 5.2.[11]

Let us briefly go through the individual points:

- The essence of it is that there is less and less evidence that prices need to be fixed. In all sectors where there is overcapacity, prices will tend to become floating. Why should a newspaper bought at 7 o'clock in the morning be sold for the

	Types of markets	
	Real markets	**Financial markets**
Price	Fixed	Floating
Knowledge of the offer	Asymmetric	Symmetric
Feedback time	Lagged	Real time
Value mindset	Stock	Flow
Source of value	Use	Trade
Regulation	Possible	Unsustainable
Risk	Eliminate through design	Adapt and hedge

Source: Davis and Meyer (1998/99), p. 109

Figure 5.2 Real markets mimic financial markets

same price as one bought at 6 in the evening? There is nothing staler than old news. Price differentiation seems the logical step. Why should all the perishable goods in a supermarket – vegetables, fruit, fish etc – be sold for the same price on the day when they are placed on the shelves fresh as one day later, when the quality has demonstrably deteriorated? Price differentiation is the answer.

- The trader's relationship with customers is no longer asymmetrical, that is hierarchical, but a relationship between equals. Symmetry is the norm in real-time markets. Customers are better informed than ever before – when was the last time you came across a customer who knew less than you? Feedback is expected in real time – we are no longer accustomed to being kept waiting.

- Values are generated by keeping everything moving and no longer by means of keeping stocks. Zara, almost a real-time business model, is a very good example of this. More than ever before, retailers try to relegate their risks to their suppliers and to pay them only when they themselves have sold the goods. Supplier-owned inventory, ie retailers only pay the supplier for the goods when they leave the store, has long been the rule in the USA and in the discount trade. If retailers sell a product within 15 days but only have to pay for them after 45 days, they earn good money.[12] Lidl is one of the champions in the hard discount trade. It has a range of almost exclusively fast-moving articles, which are sold only a few days after they are ordered, but Lidl has 30 days in which to pay the suppliers, so it can invest the gain at a profit for three weeks. It is from this perspective that Wal-Mart's power becomes most apparent. (In 2003, Wal-Mart sold around 73 per cent of its goods before payment was due to its suppliers.) Is it then surprising that customers in turn try to relegate risks to the retailer?

- The most important source of value is no longer use but trade. This is evident given the logic of today's financial markets. Can I sell the object or will it weigh down my portfolio like a lump of lead? The more potential intermediaries there are in a connected world, the more a product or a service has to have a tradability value.

- Regulation is unlikely – in other words I had better assume that the present legal framework is going to be subject to change and so I should do the deal and get out quickly.

If we summarize the main points of this outline, we can see that all the techniques and rules we know from the financial markets are tending to become relevant on the real markets. And if we look at the most important management trends of the last few years, we can see that they all follow the 'faster, better, cheaper' logic. A few examples are shown in Figure 5.3.

It is interesting to note that, from industry to trade and services right down to the final consumer, time-related strategies have become more and more significant over the last decades. We should take a closer look at some of the more important points, mainly from the service sector.

Industry	Trade	Services	Customer
Just-in-time	ECR	Yield management	'Hidden costs' strategy
Time management/ flexi-systems	CM CRM RFID	Dynamic pricing CRM Offshoring	Individually perceived added value
Outsourcing	Outsourcing		

Note: ECR = Efficient Consumer Response, CM = Category Management, CRM = Customer Relationship Management, RFID = Radio Frequency Identification

Figure 5.3 Management trends

Price

	fixed	variable
predictable	cinemas, stadiums, arenas, conference centres, leisure & entertainment parks, new retail offer	hotels, airlines, car rental, cruises
unpredictable	restaurants, golf courses, internet service providers	continuous nursing in hospitals, senior citizens' residences

Duration

Figure 5.4 Typology of revenue management

Yield management[13] was developed above all in the hospitality sector (hotel and restaurant trade) and for the airlines. In principle, yield management can be applied to all areas where there is overcapacity, particularly where there are high fixed costs and price elasticity, because in these areas customers will buy more as soon as the price falls. Here, of course, the internet has triggered a boom, as it enables access to a simple reservation system. This is particularly advantageous for airlines, which at the moment are experiencing the most extensive modernization in their entire history. Thanks to the internet reservation system with the

corresponding immediate adjustment of prices, low-price operators such as Ryanair or easyJet can say almost in real time what
capacity they have, how great the demand is at the moment,
what yields they can expect and how they have to adjust prices in
order to optimize the system. It is relevant for our purposes here
to note that, on the face of it, yield management has nothing to
do with discounting. Interestingly, however, it is now frequently
used in the hotel trade and in the airline sector as a method of
discounting. In the end, the only thing that matters to customers
is that they can get corresponding discounts by booking in
advance. And it goes without saying that anyone who comes too
late will in actual fact pay too much.

But dynamic pricing models that take the form of sophisticated
price differentials are also becoming more common in other
sectors, for example in consumer goods marketing. The most
famous example, which did the rounds in the media, was that of
the Coca-Cola vending machines with built-in sensors that adjust
the price according to the temperature outside. The warmer it
gets, the higher the price, whereas the price automatically falls
when it gets colder. There are more and more examples of price
differentials in the public sector, too, such as time-dependent tolls
on roads, for example in urban areas, tunnels etc, like the congestion charge introduced in London.[14] In order to optimize the flow
of traffic, drivers pay a charge of £5 between 7 o'clock in the
morning and 6 o'clock in the evening. This enables the city to
regulate traffic flow more effectively in peak times. In the trade
sector, dynamic pricing has not really taken hold and is still in the
initial phases. We have the so-called actionitis, a rough system of
discounts intended to bring more customers and higher average
spending per customer. However, this is more a tactical measure
than a strategic programme, as stores are introducing more and
more discounts in an attempt to offset dwindling sales figures.

The different time zones can be utilized as a means of saving
time. In a 24-hour world, the work is done wherever it happens

to be day. With today's technology, this is no problem, and so if I call my travel agency at 2 am my call is actually put through to a call centre in the USA without my noticing it. This, of course, encourages the outsourcing of simple services to other parts of the globe. We frequently see this process in action when simple, predominantly unskilled jobs are transferred to low-wage countries, though this does not have to be the case. By making use of time zones, a simple geographical outsourcing to high-wage countries can also save time and money.

To sum up this trend, we can say that there has been a general trend towards outsourcing in industry over recent years. The jobs outsourced were simple, unskilled jobs. Mainly non-strategic activities were shifted to low-wage countries, thus cutting costs. Today, the trend is quickly moving towards the outsourcing of skilled jobs in the service sector to countries offering well-trained personnel but at much lower costs.[15] Large companies make massive cost savings from the outset by shifting whole administrative processes to countries where they can get skilled personnel, particularly skilled IT personnel. The next phase after outsourcing is offshoring.[16] The difference in wage costs, for example when hiring university graduates, is tremendous. According to McKinsey, an Indian employee with a university degree costs US $3,500 per year, at least 10 to 15 times less than an American or European with the same qualifications. And because the difference in wage costs is so great, a European or American employer can afford to hire Indian personnel with much higher qualifications and negotiate ridiculously advantageous terms. If we then also take into account the above-mentioned drop in the cost of information and communication, it seems obvious that offshoring will boom in the future.

And in the end, this also contributes to making things faster.[17] Forrester Research and the US Department of Labor estimate that, between 2000 and 2005 alone, approximately 580,000 jobs will be shifted from the USA to Asia – across all sectors, from IT to sales, research, architecture, management – any job that can easily be standardized via computer and that does not require local expertise. In turn, this development also means that it is the middle income brackets that stand to lose most.

The principles of so-called yield management certainly have model character for the future. The key question is: what is the best way to harmonize service, customer, time and price when you know you have limited capacity and that this capacity can be utilized to differing degrees? The answer lies in the four Cs (see Figure 5.5): firstly, calendar (when is the booking or the sale?); secondly, clock (the timing of the rendering of the service); thirdly, capacity (depending on availability, as there will be peaks and troughs); and, finally, cost (in relation to the other factors).

Calendar: When is the booking made (or the product bought)?	Clock: Timing of the delivery of the service
Capacity: Peaks and troughs depending on availability	Cost: In relation to the other factors

Figure 5.5 The four Cs of yield management

The airline business is the most progressive here with its differentiated customer loyalty programmes ('Want miles?'), the loading factors, the reservation system and its notorious price structures. In theory, each individual passenger now flies at a different price. However, the more complex the model, the greater the number of potential errors. The airline industry is the best example of how companies can lose touch with reality and thus lose sight of the customer.[18] A similar development can be seen in the big hotel chains. Another example is the US restaurant trade. Here, the cultural differences between Anglo-Saxon and Continental European countries will probably remain evident for many years to come. While in the USA the aim is to 'sell' a table in a restaurant as many times as possible in an evening, and customers are therefore hustled through the courses of their meal and then transferred from their table to the bar, particularly in the peak time between 7 and 9 pm, such a thing would be unthinkable in Europe in a medium-class restaurant, let alone in the really upmarket establishments.

In summary:

- Time is a more abstract and thus potentially more valuable resource than money (time is non-renewable).
- The old motto 'faster, better, cheaper' remains the order of the day in mainstream business.
- The trend is towards bigger, more global, more standardized, and there is no end in sight.
- Anyone who plays this game will be forced to develop an entire information integration strategy, in other words to establish a data–knowledge–action continuum (seamless integration). This is the last possible way to be just that little bit faster than the competition – though the advantage is shrinking rapidly, as the trend follows an asymptotic curve. We spend more and more money and time on IT to eke out an ever-dwindling advantage in time.[19]
- Real markets mimic financial markets – but financial markets are driven by human nature. This means we can expect increasingly frequent accidents on the real markets, too. Catastrophes are logical, become a matter of course and will increase in frequency.

The neglect of personal resources: the logic of increase means higher hidden costs for the customer

For customers, too, the time factor is increasingly important. To put it bluntly, the manufacturers, retailers and service providers are getting quite cheeky. The euphemism 'customer orientation' conceals the fact that they are bent on passing on as many costs as possible to the customer. It is not simply a matter of price, though the price is and will remain an important factor. Price and value have become even more dominant. However, we tend to overlook the so-called 'hidden costs', which include all the costs we incur even before we have decided what we want. We try to inform ourselves as far as possible. We read brochures, put up with the most awful advertising blurb and fight our way along supermarket aisles to find what we are looking for. We expend physical energy, drive to stores to look at products, hunt for parking spaces, pay exorbitant parking fees a lot of the time, pay for the depreciation in the value of our cars, push trolleys and wait in queues at the checkout. And we don't charge the supplier a penny for any of this. Why not? By the time a family has decided whether to do its shopping in town or locally, a lot of physical and mental energy has been expended. And these rising costs don't appear anywhere in any profit and loss account. Why not? Studies such as that carried out by Henley in Britain – a country where this development has progressed much further than in Germany or France – confirm that there is increasing differentiation in this field and that people invest much more of their personal resources than ever before (see Figure 5.6).

Of those asked, 60 per cent stated that they did not have enough money and 58 per cent think they have 'just enough' space available. Despite increases in efficiency, our personal resources are being depleted.

Personal resources: too much/just enough/too little

Time:	10 / 43 / 47%
Energy:	4 / 42 / 55%
Space:	7 / 58 / 35%
Money:	2 / 38 / 60%

Figure 5.6   Availability of personal resources

Let us take a brief look at the individual factors:

- *Time.* In many areas, prices and costs are falling, thanks to the axis of evil. But that is only one side of things. If we take a closer look, we will see that there is a dramatic increase in the cost in terms of time. Holidays may be getting cheaper and cheaper, with low-price flights and hotels, but it takes us longer and longer to decide where we want to go. Should we go to Ibiza, Majorca or Rimini or should we just visit family again? There has been a drastic increase in the cost of looking for and gathering information, and of orientation and communication. These are not evaluated and entered in a balance sheet like true costs. We can quote various US and European sources on the subject of this phenomenon – they all reached basically the same conclusion.[20] More than half of all Europeans feel that they do not have enough time. The more time is seen as something that is in short supply, the more people are willing to pay for it – voluntarily or involuntarily.

  We measure status by how people spend their time. In the evolution of consumption, it has replaced conspicuous consumption as the dominant theme. More and more consumers now count seconds as if they were superfluous calories instead of wanting to drive a more expensive and more elegant car than the people next door.

This fits in perfectly with the results of a study conducted by BMW in 2003, which found that Germans today spend an average of 200 days of their life in traffic jams, and the figure is likely to rise. If we differentiate between premium customers and discount customers we can say that the premium customer is willing to spend money in order to save time, while the discount customer spends time in order to save money.

If we look at a possible division of consumers into customer segments, we will see that, next to price, time has probably become the most important criterion in customer segmentation. Taking just the two criteria of time and price gives us a much more differentiated picture and one that is much more precise than the traditional patterns.[21] However, there are other criteria that can be taken into consideration to round off the picture.

- *Physical and mental energy.* Our desires and our opportunities are growing faster than our ability to use them. The greatest problem of consumer democracy is that consumers are no longer in a position to reap its benefits. We have reached our physical and mental limits. Customers are overstressed and over-informed. Many young people complain that they have 'had enough'. Weary of it all, people stay at home and eat leftovers from the fridge because they are fed up with looking for parking spaces or studying cinema programmes. People find that activities such as housework, shopping for their everyday requirements or investigating possible invest-ments on the internet sap their energy more and more. The yearning for simplicity and relief is increasing exponentially.
- *Space.* The richer we become, the more space we need and the more space becomes a factor we are prepared to pay for. Houses, hotel reception areas and working space have to increase in size for us to feel comfortable. All too often, customers today find that they just don't have the space to

store the economy-size box of cornflakes. Our balconies, cellars and cupboards are full to overflowing. Customers are not only over-informed and overstressed; they also have too much stuff. And so an increasing number of people are willing – though perhaps not completely voluntarily – to pay for space, if only for a short time, for example in a restaurant, where they will be prepared to pay more for a meal because the tables are a little further apart. For this reason, things like new loft and lounge concepts, members-only clubs, VIP treatment etc are going to become increasingly important.

This leads to new clusters into which consumers can be segmented (see Figure 5.7). There are people who are rich in time and space but poor in energy and money – such as people performing manual labour. There are people who are rich in energy and time, but poor in money, for example many senior citizens. Many people are rich in information, but poor in energy and time. These include many members of the traditional middle classes in intellectual professions. A growing number of people are poor in all resources. And a relatively large number are rich in all resources – those with good pensions or the surviving parasites of the New Economy. All this means that, if we are moving towards a

Eternal students, senior citizens without savings, eco-types	lots of time and little money	lots of time and lots of money	Rich pensioners, those who married rich, lottery winners, parasites of the New Economy
Managers, businesspeople, families with double incomes	little time and lots of money	little time and little money	The working poor, low-income families

Figure 5.7 The fastest-growing customer segments

real-time economy, we are going to have to be prepared constantly to re-examine and readjust these segmentations.

In the field of marketing, these personal resources have so far been woefully neglected. But to get a more differentiated picture of the service element of trade, we must look at all the effort customers put in before they decide to buy a product. We suggest the following definition:

> Profitability of personal resources = Maximization of personal customer value for time and productivity by reducing the cost of time and stress and financial costs in the customer's life.

Thus, we have to realize that customers do much more than simply spend money or carry out business transactions. They invest in personal resources! Before they buy, they invest time, information, space and physical and mental energy. If we fail to understand these processes that take place prior to a sale, we will never understand developed markets. A company that can offer less stress, more simplicity and more time- and cost-saving potential will be a winner without having to make any particular effort in other areas!

It is interesting to note that we have reached very different stages of cultural and national development. Good examples are the food service markets. Whereas in Britain or the USA the time factor has long been recognized as a service that is integrated into products, Germany lags at least five to eight years behind in this respect. And we can see the same pattern if we arrange restaurant types according to the criteria of time and money.

So – to give just a few main examples – we will continue to work on these hidden costs and generate new packages to offer our customers in the following areas:

- a new definition of convenience (less time spent searching, more orientation, general savings in time);

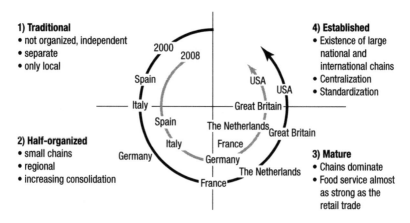

Figure 5.8 Time markets food/restaurant typology (development from 2000 to 2008)

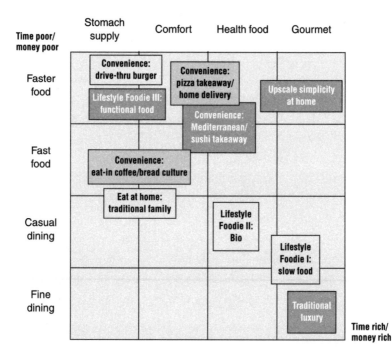

Figure 5.9 Forms of eating

- further development of the comfort theme (the good feeling of familiarity, atmosphere, ease – for example comfort food);
- a re-evaluation of connectivity (a feeling of being linked up in a simple way or the feeling of belonging to certain communities etc).

Eating can take many forms, from quickly filling your stomach at low cost to an opulent dinner. The trend is towards more large, centrally organized chains and fewer family restaurants.

Differentiation logic (Logic No. 2): what happens when uncontrollable costs of side-effects exceed costs

The logic of increase is a Bladerunner logic, as it means you are implementing a high-risk strategy socially and economically. We learn that 'faster, better, cheaper' generates higher and higher incidental costs, which in the end are uncontrollable. It is not possible to integrate all three elements – faster, better and cheaper.

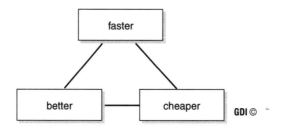

Figure 5.10   The logic of increase: 'more of the same'

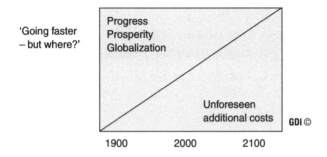

Figure 5.11 Incidental costs and prosperity

So we see now that it is possible to combine only two of these elements – faster, better and cheaper – successfully. Any attempt to achieve all three aims at the same time, as in the logic of increase, will lead inevitably to things like BSE, notorious epidemic diseases, child labour in the Philippines or Indonesia, illegal working conditions such as those often to be seen in emerging nations, exaggerated developments on the stock markets, and ecological catastrophes. The three elements cannot even be combined in the IT sector. I can make the hardware faster, better, cheaper, but at the same time this makes the software more vulnerable, more overladen, slower. We have to limit ourselves, to make a choice,[22] because the increasing likelihood of incurring the cost of incidental effects in our faster-better-cheaper world means that we are accumulating uncontrollable losses. And we know all too well what that means: the profits are privatized and the losses nationalized.

Let us examine what this means by taking a look at a present-day example: US eating habits, which have been revolutionized in recent years by the fast food world. In a food world that functions according to the principle 'faster, better, cheaper' but that is part of a larger, complex and dynamic context, people are steadily gaining weight.[23] And the increase is exponential, not linear. If the development continues at the present pace, around 40 per cent of Americans (68 million people) will be obese – not simply overweight – by 2010. Today, 31 per cent are obese. And the number of people who are extremely obese (100 or more pounds over a healthy weight) increased fourfold between 1986 and 2000. That means 4 million Americans today are extremely obese. The Behavioral Medicine Research Center at the Baylor College of Medicine in Houston has calculated that, if this development continues and eating habits do not change, every American will be overweight or obese by the year 2040! And as a cause of death, obesity is far more common than acts of terror or war. The reason for this increase in weight is simple: the size of portions in the entire food sector has steadily increased. And people eat faster than ever before, usually while performing a multitude of other tasks at the same time. Moreover, nowhere in the Western world is food more readily available. People are encouraged to eat everywhere they go. It is already a fact that over 20 per cent of meals in the United States are eaten in the car.[24] And nowhere in the Western world is food cheaper. Ronald Shaich, CEO of the bread chain Panera Bread, says of fast food restaurants: 'They've all become self-service gasoline stations for the human body.'[25] More is more: if you order a soft drink in a restaurant today, the smallest quantity you can get is a litre. Fast food restaurants offer 'free refills', so you can drink as much Coke as you want. The margins are so exorbitant that they can easily afford it if customers drink two litres of Coke or Sprite with their Whopper or Big Mac. And the portions are getting bigger – as mentioned before, Americans stretch everything, from meat portions to limousines. Portions, whether of soft drinks, fries, hamburgers or crisps, are apparently now twice as large as they were 20 years ago.[26] What paradoxical behavioural effects this can produce was illustrated, for example, by a study on girls' individual perception of their own weight. In all weight classes, more than one-third of the girls said they considered themselves overweight. In reality, however, only between 6 per cent and 8 per cent of them were.[27] And the result is a behavioural pattern that leads to weight gain.

We can summarize the differential logic as shown in Figure 5.12.

Faster + better → more expensive

Better + cheaper → slower

Faster + cheaper → worse

Figure 5.12   Differential logic

We just can't have 'faster, better *and* cheaper' – unless we are prepared to accept the increasing incidental cost. We will have to be satisfied with the combination of just two of these elements. This is true of the food sector – where it is perhaps most obvious – but also of biotechnology or the air travel sector. You want faster and better – you can have it, but it will be more expensive. When the discounters have finally driven the air travel sector to ruin and existing structures have been destroyed, the discount operators themselves, with their skilful yield management techniques, will finally liquidate themselves. Faster and cheaper means worse. Up to a certain degree, we can carry on as we are now for some years, for example if there are sufficient resources. And the discounters are exploiting that fact, and who can blame them? This applies in greatly varying degrees, however, to greatly varying raw materials. Above all, the steadily increasing incidental costs have to be borne by someone. At the moment, we all bear them. And finally, if we want to be better and cheaper, it is a simple fact that processes will be very slow.

So, in conclusion, we can say that time will not so easily become a freely available commodity. Time is the resource that is in shortest supply, and it is a non-renewable resource. So time and luxury will inevitably become linked – our yearning for the timeless, the classic, will grow. The difference between 'made' products and 'grown' products will become increasingly important, because the latter are rarer and therefore more desirable. In our overabundance of information, those products we call classics will be seen as particularly desirable. Classic products are timeless and have achieved a certain status in the course of time – they have become valuable, they were not manipulated to be so. Their history makes them high-quality products. While, for example, new wines are developed at a rapid pace in California or Australia or South Africa and sold with the help of vast marketing budgets, wines in which consumers quickly lose interest, you cannot re-create a Château Latour or Domaine de la Romanée Conti. Without wanting to praise these wines, it can be said that in the end they exert a stronger attraction because they are anchored in the collective consciousness and have usually acquired a mythical character. They can only escape our awareness for a while and then be rediscovered again. 'Created' wines cannot compete with this status.

And when 'faster, better, cheaper' reaches its limits, 'bigger, more global, more standardized' will also be hampered in its potential for growth or at least in its profit-making potential. Nothing will be more exciting than to observe the further development of the pacesetter Wal-Mart.

In conclusion: what do the time factor and the hidden costs for the customer mean for the Age of Cheap? We have to admit that the discount managers are as a rule excellent time managers. As a result of the rationalization measures described in Chapter 4, they are very well equipped for the battles to come. On the customer side, too, they manage to cut many of the hidden costs. And without even attempting to take money for the service.

Notes

[1] Quoted from *NYT Magazine*, 24 November 2002, p 72.
[2] This is the motto of James H Gilmore and B Joseph Pine II in their classic work (1999) *The Experience Economy*, Harvard Business School Press, Boston, MA.

3   On the subject of the localization of 'faster' trends within today's megatrends and basic trends in the economy and society, see David Bosshart and Karin Frick (2003) 'Megatrends basic: 7 megatrends und gegentrends', GDI study.

4   See James Gleick (1999) *Faster: The acceleration of just about everything*, Pantheon, New York.

5   In this respect, too, we are becoming more Americanized. See the wonderful books by Harvard lecturer and critic of consumerism Juliet Schor: *The Overspent American: Upscaling, downshifting and the new consumer*, Basic Books, New York, 1998; and *Do Americans Shop Too Much?*, Beacon Press, Boston, MA, 2000. The counterpart is of course the overworked American; see *The Overworked American: The unexpected decline of leisure*, Basic Books, New York, 1992. These books describe a programme of downshifting. On this subject, see *The Overspent American*, pp 111ff.

6   See Richard D'Aveni (1994) *Hypercompetition: Managing the dynamics of strategic maneuvering*, Free Press, New York.

7   See the excellent book from the Ernst & Young Center for Business Innovation: Stan Davis and Christopher Meyer (1998/99) *Blur: The speed of change in the connected economy*, Capstone, Reading, especially pp 96–110.

8   On the subject of this phenomenon in its political and economic significance, see the works of Jean-Jacques Rosa, especially *Le Second XXe Siècle: Déclin des hiérarchies et avenir des nations*, Grasset Economie, Paris, 2000, especially pp 237–308.

9   There is no room here to go into this subject in depth. See the classic work by Peter Buckley and Jonathan Michie (eds) (1996) *Firms, Organizations and Contracts: A reader in industrial organisation*, Oxford University Press, Oxford.

10 For an analysis of the link between networking, the global economy and the financial markets, see Loretta Napoleoni (2003) *Modern Jihad: Tracing the dollars behind the terror networks*, Pluto Press, London; for a political and strategic analysis, see Pierre Hassner (2003) *La Terreur et L'Empire: La violence et la paix*, II, Seuil, Paris, especially p 147.

11 See Stan Davis and Christopher Meyer (1998/99) *Blur: The speed of change in the connected economy*, Capstone, Reading, p 103.

12 See John L Stanton (2002) 'Here comes another paradigm breaker', *Food Processing*, November, p 22.

13 For many years, the leading authority on the development of yield management has been Cornell University, The Center for Hospitality Research. See for example Cathy A Enz and Glenn Witham (2001) *CHR Reports*, Cornell University, Ithaca, NY.

[14] See 'Congestion charging: Ken Livingstone's gamble', *Economist*, 15 February 2003, pp 37–39; also Chris Giles and Juliette Jowitt (2003) 'As London launches its congestion charging experiment, gridlocked cities around the world watch with interest', *Financial Times*, 13 February, p 9.

[15] See also Chapter 2, 'White-collar offshoring – the migration of high-quality services to low-wage countries'.

[16] There is a rapid increase in the literature on and research into this subject. Once again, such trends appear first in the Anglo-Saxon countries, while Continental Europe hangs back, which may not be so unwise, as it allows a better understanding of the above-mentioned 'hidden costs'.

[17] See, for example, Michelle Kessler and Stephanie Armour (2003) 'USA has a disturbing export: white-collar jobs', *USA Today*, 5 August, pp 7, 7A.

[18] Perhaps the best work on customer orientation as illustrated by the airline sector is by none other than Henry Mintzberg (2001): *Why I Hate Flying: Tales for the tormented traveller*, Texere, New York. The book begins with a sarcastic warning to the reader (p V): 'Many of the experiences reported in this book occurred in an earlier millenium. Corporations make progress. Things have probably gotten worse.'

[19] But once again, our sums won't add up, as there is a further paradox here: the more IT solves problems and seemingly eases the load on us, the greater the problems that IT cannot solve, ie human problems.

[20] Perhaps one of the best, wittiest and most perceptive books on this subject was written by James Gleick; see Note 4.

[21] Alan Mitchell's outstanding book (2001), *Right Side Up: Building brands in the age of the organized consumer*, HarperCollins, London, offers a wealth of arguments.

[22] There is no convergence of development. 'There is a reverse Moore's Law… As processors become faster and memory becomes cheaper, software becomes correspondingly slower and more bloated, using up all available resources.' Jaron Lanier, *Wired*, 12/2000.

[23] This subject has been examined in detail. The conclusions reached are always the same, even if the statistics vary owing to the different methods of calculation used. Interesting recent research reports include that of the Center for Disease Control and Prevention, the Rand Corporation or the North American Association for the Study of Obesity.

[24] According to Professor Christopher Muller, Chair for Multiunit Restaurant Management, University of Central Florida, Orlando.

[25] Quoted in *USA Today*, 30 September 2002, p 2.

[26] According to calculations made by USA Today Research, *USA Today*, 14 October 2003, p 1.

[27] According to the Center for Disease Control and Prevention, 'Youth risk behavior surveillance 2001'.

6 No frills

On the illusions of the service economy

What is at the core of the Age of Cheap? We have dealt in detail with the close connection between excess, superfluity and discount and the resulting insoluble economic and moral paradox. A further step that will enable us to gain a closer insight into the Age of Cheap is to ask ourselves what is the connection between it and the promises of our service economy. After all, we do still claim to be living in a service economy. To put it bluntly, the Age of Cheap is also an answer to the practical impossibility of achieving a service world.

'Outsourcing to the customer': the myths of services

In an increasingly global economy, the world of services simply becomes too expensive. Only a few can afford it. To put it more radically, there is no real service economy. No one knows exactly what services are, unless the definition is kept very broad.[1] If we take the problem of hidden costs (see Chapter 5), we would be justified in maintaining that Aldi is an excellent provider of service, because it attains clarity of range, has strong in-store orientation, makes a pre-selection of articles and offers low prices. Hardly any other retailer can cut hidden costs to the customer to such an extent.

However, it is an equally important fact that no one seems willing to pay voluntarily for services. The so-called tertiary sector is more and more of an illusion. The more complex and opaque the world of products becomes, the greater the probability that customers will prefer to buy what they feel more comfortable with: a product that they understand minus the service that they are not really sure will benefit them anyway. In the vast majority of cases, it seems, customers want 'net' goods. The only form of service that really works is self-service, that is, a company's skilful outsourcing to the customer of anything that is critical or delicate in its relationship with its customers. Only companies that succeed in transferring as much as possible to the customers, in getting them to do as much as possible themselves, will be successful. The IT sector or the automobile sector are very good examples of this. The more complex the form in which the world of goods presents itself to us, the more of an illusion it is to believe that people are prepared to pay for complex services – unless, of course, one has a monopoly or is working in a area like health care where the customer's motivation is fear. In these areas, it will probably be possible to continue making obscene profits in future. But these areas are more the exception than the rule. Even the banks – think of personal banking – are facing major changes. What about services in hotels, in restaurants and in tourism? US tipping practice shows just how dishonest the whole situation is. I am expected always to add 15 or even more per cent to the bill, even if the service was mediocre. This has more to do with a mechanical forced economy than with an economy in which services are appreciated and then rewarded accordingly.

Seen from this angle, the McDonald's concept is also inconsistent. Euphemistically, they promise in a recent advertising slogan, 'We do it all for you.' A more realistic version would be: 'We do it all for them.' We, the customers, do everything: we wait in a queue, sigh and grind our teeth. We pick up the product ourselves; it is not brought to the table for us. We carry it. We clear away afterwards. We inform ourselves instead of asking a waiter for information. And to top it all, we pay for everything. There is no gradation and no transparency. One customer is lucky and does not have to wait. Another is unlucky – these things happen – and has to stand in the queue for 15 minutes. But everyone pays the same price. The Easy concept from Stelios is more customer-friendly because, there, I know that I am getting a good deal, that I can save more and more, because I myself am in control – for example, I can book a room under the easyDorm system, making use of the hotel concept. The more I do for myself – clearing up the room, making up the beds myself etc – the less I pay. And if I hire a car from easyCar and wash it before I return it, I pay less too. So it is hardly surprising that 90 per cent of the cars are returned clean. To say it again quite clearly, what Stelios Haji-Ioannou calls 'outsourcing to the customer'[2] is the key to successful low-price operations. For the concept to work, customers have to be willing to go along with it and, above all, they have to understand the product. If customers have no idea what they are letting themselves in for, they will not play along with the outsourcing idea – which, after all, is an insourcing for them! And so this model does hold promise: I know exactly what is on offer. I know exactly what I'm getting and, much more importantly, because the expectations are so clearly defined I also know exactly what I'm not getting.

Another idea that follows the same general aim is called 'added value' in present-day marketing jargon. There has been a lot of talk about 'customer delight'. You have to offer your customers added value, as much added value as possible. Keep piling on the added value to keep your customer delighted. This drives expectations to an unbelievable, almost magical extreme. It was at best well meant, but it has not done anything to produce a clear definition of what exactly is being offered. The supplier no longer knows what added value to offer, and the customer doesn't know exactly what to expect, and so the endless pursuit of added value has led to many unnecessary costs. The result is usually unproductive creativity, and people lose sight of what is possible. This is also very unpleasant for employees, who then have to deal with the false expectations of frustrated customers.

You don't have to be a prophet to see that, in the Age of Cheap, suppliers who limit themselves to providing what is reasonable and necessary will have the competitive edge. They can satisfy their customers' expectations and keep costs under control. With the growing influence of the internet, potential customer power is slowly but steadily increasing. Customers are better informed and their expectations become more refined, so that in many cases they need no additional information from the supplier. The more the internet becomes a good, cheap and fast source of information, the more efficiently customers can find out all they want to know about a product and then simply go out and buy it from the supplier. This aspect gives customers the pleasant feeling that they are making their own choices and defining their own terms. And with increasing transparency, more and more customers ask: do I really want to pay more? Do I need an added-value service when I am better off paying the 'net' price? If – as described in Chapter 3 on Wal-Mart – an easy source of information tells me that I can get a famous Opus One wine 30 per cent cheaper at Wal-Mart than from a wine dealer, I am only too happy to dispense with any further services round this cult wine. The simple fact that I can save so much money makes me happy, and I am more than willing to do without the trimmings: the attractive displays, the designer store, the personal service etc.

It is not a question of under-expecting or over-delivering or over-execution. It is all about clarity of expectations and the precise fulfilment of these expectations. The rest follows automatically. To say it again: constantly trying to exceed the customers' expectations is much more risky; it confuses things, and mutual discontent is the result.

If we assume that the above-mentioned hidden costs are going to continue to increase, then the desire for simplicity, comprehensibility and orientation is also going to increase. The titles of bestselling books like *An Idiot's Guide to...*, *... for Dummies*, *Simplify your Life*, *Simple Things*, *Simple Life* or *Management the Simple Way*, to mention just a few, speak volumes. This trend has long taken hold in all areas of knowledge and human activity. It is also no coincidence that Dieter Schwanitz's books on education and general knowledge have been such a success – *All You Need to Know* (to hold your own in intellectual conversation) is an invaluable guide to help me strip off all the intellectual ballast. Or the magazine *Real Simple*, which was launched last year, aims to teach us how to rid our lives of all the things we don't need in order to be happy. To make it clear here: this is not a criticism of the consumer society in general but a criticism of the fact that it is impossible to reap the fruits of this abundance of offers in a sensible and appropriate way. What we need is not more and more of the same, but something different.[3] With increasing price orientation, products are going to become more and more interchangeable. The more the growing army of suppliers hawk their wares with the same message, the louder the background din will become and the less likely it is that differentiated messages will be heard.

If we look at the history of this development and see it in relation to the 'faster, better, cheaper' trend, we can identify three phases over the last 50 years (see Figure 6.1).

From 1950 to 1970, the motto was obligation: modest consumption to satisfy your needs. Don't spend money before you've got it. But between 1970 and 1990, the array of goods and services consumers could choose from exploded. As trade expanded to become regional, then national and then

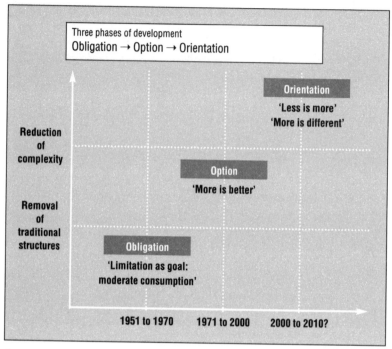

Source: GDI

Figure 6.1   Obligation, option and orientation

international, there were more innovations and more products
to choose from on the shelves. Consumers were faced with ever-
increasing options, and consumer expectations changed step by
step to keep pace with the possibilities offered. If I can get three
TV channels, there's nothing I want more than to be able to
watch 10. When I can watch 10, I want 20. When I have 20
channels to choose from, I find it perfectly normal that the next
day they are offering me 30. But when I can get 50 or 60 different channels, the situation changes. I don't really watch TV any
more; I just zap around trying not to miss anything. And at the
end of the evening, I'm frustrated because I haven't really
watched a single programme. It is then increasingly likely that I
won't turn the TV set on at all. So we can see that, from a

certain quantitative optimum point onwards, there is a qualitative leap that alters our behaviour. We can transfer the example of the TV channels to many other product segments and see the same development. If a supermarket introduces a new range of preserves at a special introductory price, the consumer reaction is as follows: with a range of 24 flavours, the supermarket attracts 60 per cent more customers, whereas, if it has only six flavours to choose from, only 40 per cent more people will come to the store. If the supermarket looks at how much it actually sells, the picture is a very different one: with a range of 24 flavours, only 3 per cent of customers will buy. If they have only six flavours to choose from, 30 per cent of customers will buy a jar. We can conclude from this that we have now reached the third phase – what people need today is not more options, but more orientation. And the question is: if there are 50 or 60 TV channels, how many of them are still profitable? And how many of the hundred different TV programme guides are still making money?

There appear to be two important insights here. When people have too many options, they become confused. They think that they are missing something important. They become inefficient and dissatisfied. And if they are confronted with a situation where they have no options at all, no alternatives, then they react with aggression. That is exactly what we are seeing with the opponents of globalization, and the most impressive demonstration of this was the terrorist attacks of 11 September 2001.

So the path for the future must be 'less is more' or 'more is different'. This means a shift in attitudes from 'too much' to 'less'. The question is no longer 'What else can I do?' but 'What can I do without? What don't I need any more? What don't I need to know?' Here, too, the message is: people don't want to buy or consume less; what they want is to buy or consume differently.

In short, swamping the customer with 'too much' not only has negative consequences on subjective consumer mood, but it also has a direct negative effect on sales:

- Too many options, overabundant ranges and a profusion of products that are all more or less the same only produce confusion and lessen the attraction.
- Where ranges are smaller, customers feel more empowered and buy more than when they have endless supermarket aisles of equal products to choose from. The all-important question is: does the range or the supplier dictate what I do, or do I have the power because I am in the picture? Only the latter promises success for the customer and profit for the supplier.

So if there are still services in the future, they will be predominantly on the level of a reduction of hidden costs. They will hinge on the above-mentioned values of convenience, comfort and connectivity. What gives me mental and physical energy? What gives me a feeling of comfort and security? What gives me the feeling that I am on top of things? What gives me the feeling that I have used my time profitably? The result will be more attention to detail and the following phenomena, which can already be observed here and there on our planet:

- Traffic lights for pedestrians and motorists will no longer simply switch colour, but will count down the time left in seconds until they change colour on a display. Letting stressed-out pedestrians waiting at the lights know that they will be able to continue on their way in just 15, 14, 13 seconds is a simple but effective way to reduce stress.
- The omnipresent canned music in airports, lifts, department stores and waiting rooms will change from hip hop or hard rock to classical music. Vivaldi and Bach give me more energy; AC/DC or the Rolling Stones sap it. We know that

customers in wine departments of stores stay longer and buy more expensive wines when classical music is playing in the background. Hard rock or techno drives them out of the shop more quickly, and they buy lower-priced wines.

So it is not simply a question of reducing the number of articles available, optimizing category management or providing an extra checkout. The message is: simplify the shopping experience! Only customers who have the feeling they have invested their time profitably will be loyal.

Having come to a rather sobering conclusion with regard to the future development of services, another question that arises is: what does this mean for customer orientation? The dominant ideology of the 1990s was customer orientation. But who really takes care of the customer? Is it not a fact that, in our increasingly individualistic, if not autistic, world, it is not the customer who is the focus of attention, but taking care of number one? If we look at priorities, isn't career orientation more important than customer orientation? And if we have the choice between making a sale and serving the customer well, isn't sales orientation more important? And if we take it further: profit orientation or sales orientation? Isn't profit orientation more important? Playing with ideas – albeit seriously – in this way reveals how irrelevant the customer is in actual fact.

Marketing means selling goods: the myth of customer orientation

The outstanding work of Stephen Brown, perhaps the only interesting and innovative professor of marketing, sums it all up: marketing means selling the customer your product.[4] No ifs and buts. When customers are better informed than suppliers, when marketing strategies are so transparent that even a child can see through them, there is a new sobriety. Customers buy what you offer them. And if they don't want it, they won't buy it. As we have said before, every customer is a B2B customer. Marketing is a parody of itself. The constant bombardment of customers with marketing messages has led to a situation where the customer sees through the farce, finds the messages a nuisance and over-exaggerates or ironizes them. In our world of overabundance, customers have also developed a healthy 'marketing reflex'. We once visited a luxury restaurant that had been awarded several stars with our then seven-year-old daughter. The staff were very friendly and attentive and gave her a teddy bear. Our daughter looked at me and said: 'Daddy, we've already paid for it, haven't we?' The crux of the matter is that, of course, she was delighted with this present and thanked the staff politely. But because of the 'marketing reflex', she also automatically and pragmatically saw through the gesture. So customers are quite happy to have the wool pulled over their eyes. In fact, they love tricks and appreciate the wittiness of marketing – but they know how the trick is done. And so the core of the matter is the marketing of marketing. How do marketers market their marketing?

Advertising loses its innocence because we have learned to automatically look behind the scenes. The successful Diesel campaign is probably the best example of how to play with customers who are intelligent enough to play with the marketing messages themselves. 'Consumers are like roaches. We spray them with marketing and for a time it works. Then inevitably they develop an immunity, a resistance.'[5] The most important insight, one that we have forgotten in recent years, is that 'There is no such thing as a free lunch.' 'Free lunch' is a reference to the pretzels and potato crisps placed on the bar for customers to help themselves to. The pretzels and crisps are free, but appear-ances are deceptive: the 'free' lunch is salty and therefore makes you thirsty. And that old evergreen, 'authenticity', has lost its meaning too. That original, authentic Italian mountain restaurant has been designed to look authentic. Free-range hens roam free, but their surroundings are squalid. And Grandmother's original-recipe pasta is produced industrially. You can try to evoke the impression of authenticity, try to emphasize authenticity – but the same applies as to advertising slogans in general: as all the slogans that mean anything have already been invented and can now only be repeated, we have a situation that Umberto Eco described as the typical communication dilemma. How can I, as a man, assure a woman of my undying love when generations of romantic authors have said it so perfectly before, when the words have been repeated so often that they have lost their meaning? All that remains is cliché. The only option left is to make a last attempt at authenticity, look the woman in the eye and say 'As Barbara Cartland would put it, "I will love you for ever."'

We can put it like this: 'It is possible to become too customer-oriented and marketing is rapidly heading that way. We have got so close to consumers that we're breathing down their necks.'[6] You don't have to despise your customers, but neither is it productive to take them as seriously as mainstream ideology in marketing would have had us do in recent decades. Listening to customers, wooing them, can also be fatal. In an economy where everyone engages in benchmarking, in which marketing messages are omnipresent, the more we try to understand the customer, the more banal the result and the less consumer interest we will arouse. And this shows us that, in this respect too, the low-price operators are better equipped for the marketing battles of the future, where the plain and simple objective will be 'Sell!'

In most cases, well-meant customer orientation leads to customer disorientation.[7] Stephen Brown's model or anti-model 'The dozen Ds of customer disorientation'[8] describes it perfectly and sums it all up:

Disregarding the customer increases their Desire.
Denying the customer increases their Determination.

Depriving the customer increases their Desperation.
Deferring customer consummation drives them to Distraction.
Delivering the goods or services inspires Devotion.
Desisting immediately induces Disorientation.

And when Brown comments ironically on his anti-model, he is perfectly well aware that he can do so only by adhering to the language of marketing. Yet this anti-model probably tells us more than all the books on marketing and communication published in the last few decades. It offers a sobering insight into the reality of today's markets.

So, equally soberly, we can say that in Britain – just think of London, where service is in theory valued above anything else – we pay for the over-politeness of sales personnel with very high margins. And in the USA, we pay for a hurriedly rehearsed pattern of sales ritual. Unlike the European countries, which had a long and above all aristocratic and monarchic tradition, the USA first had to create a service culture and the corresponding rituals. This explains why, in the USA, the immediate focus is on selling, and the best (and most shameless) example of this is Las Vegas: marketing in its raw and unadulterated form. Everything the customer has to put up with is hyperbole. However, there is something incredibly liberating in this. In Austria, for example – just think of Vienna – there is a lot of baroque sidetracking. As a customer, you play along with the age-old rituals and everything proceeds at a cultured and leisurely pace, but you pay for it in the end. In France, the burden of military tradition is omnipresent and can be felt in an eloquent but stiff marketing that bears witness to the basic contempt traditionally exhibited towards those who are still forced to earn their living and have not yet received unspoken absolution from the powers that be. Germany, with its legendary thoroughness, is the most progressive country in this respect. There is a lot of talk there about the importance of customer orientation – culminating in the debate about 'service desert Germany'. But at the same time, hard discounters in Germany demonstrate day by day what customer orientation has in actual fact long been. As the Germans lack the more subtle 'quiet desperation' of the English, they make no pretence at being over-polite. The Germans simply want to sell their products. They are convinced that they have the best product, which is a great advantage – see the automobile industry. You can err too far in the other direction, however – see the German railway company Deutsche Bahn. If the product is not right and has absolutely no relevance whatsoever to customer requirements, then you will not boost sales. And the Swiss, semi-isolated and a little nervous, remain caught up in their somewhat naïve domestic market mentality. They are still labouring under the illusion that high quality alone can guarantee survival. The people most well equipped for the battles of the future are probably the Italians, who have the unbelievable image boost provided by their popular and coveted way of life – Pizza! Pasta! Panini! With their strong but gentle theatrical manner, they make a direct appeal to the consumer soul with their *emozioni*. In this age of omnipresent marketing, the Italians are selling more and more even though we are aware of the dark threat of the Mafia and other obscure aspects.

Notes

1   It is no coincidence that there is still no good standard book on the subject of service.
2   Stelios introduced the concept at the 4th European Foodservice Summit in Zurich, 25–26 September 2003.
3   See GDI-Impuls No. 1/02, dedicated to the subject of 'Simpler but better'. See there David Bosshart, 'Einfacher einkaufen – einfacher leben', pp 16–23.
4   See Stephen Brown (2003) *Free Gift Inside! Forget the customer: develop marketease*, Capstone, West Sussex. See also his earlier work (1995) *Postmodern Marketing*, Routledge, London, which gives a very theoretical, but sound and interesting, overview of a different approach to marketing theories.

5 Jonathan Bond and Richard Kirshenbaum (1998) *Under the Radar: Talking to today's cynical consumer*, John Wiley, New York, p 92.

6 Source as cited above, p 10.

7 At the University of St Gallen, Institute of Trade and Marketing, a dissertation is being written on the subject of 'Customer confusion', a very relevant subject in our day.

8 Brown, *Free Gift Inside!*, p 57.

7 What is worth what?

Prices in the Age of Cheap

We know the price of everything and the value of nothing.

Oscar Wilde

Today, we compare everything with everything else. Economy and society are rapidly heading towards real time. With the density of networks in the virtual world approaching that of the human brain, dynamism and complexity increase exponentially. Any status quo becomes merely the present configuration of a kaleidoscopic and ever-changing pattern. It follows that price or price orientation will become increasingly important for both suppliers and customers, and price competence will become the key competence for all suppliers.[1] If you lose control of the price, you lose the most important strategic tool enabling you to operate profitably and survive.

Increasing pressure for liberalization, the removal of trade barriers and the availability of better information mean that the significance of time as a competitive edge is dwindling. The Global Village means Global Pillage. If you have a good product, you will make the most you can of it as quickly as possible, because a (cheaper) copy will be in the shops tomorrow. Suppliers today know that all they can hope for is temporary monopolies. A connected world is under continual stress and there are few pauses for breath.

To ensure prosperity on a higher level, we have to play the game. The richer a nation is, the more difficult this is to understand and follow. When you've got it all, it's hard to explain the necessity for keeping on running. The '15 minutes of fame' that Andy Warhol demanded for everyone have long become a basic goal for all participants in the media-dominated world. Products, people, services, institutions, nations, brands – they all want their 15 minutes of fame. And the aim is to generate as much capital for the future as possible in this brief and extraordinary situation. For companies, this is the phase of 'obscene profits'. And of course television, as a medium that tries to focus attention despite the increasing impossibility of the task, has to provide this temporary limelight. The who-wants-to-be-a-millionaire games, the game shows and the dating shows give the candidates their 15 minutes of fame and the chance to generate enough capital to provide for their future.

An increasingly connected world means easy access to information and thus a high degree of interaction. No one wants to be left out. But the wide variety of wishes leaves no room for concerted long-term campaigns. A myriad values and wishes clamour for fulfilment and realization. Anyone who has to stand in a queue will get impatient and start pushing if the queue isn't moving fast enough. So it becomes necessary to have a widely varying and highly flexible range of offers, which in turn necessitates a constant supply of ever-changing fads to keep the markets buzzing. This is the only way to ensure ongoing progress at a high level and enable a company to keep abreast of developments. It means that, without many variations in offers and a never-ending succession of '15 minutes of fame' and with a simultaneous high increase in the number of disappointments, the economic system will not achieve overall flexibility and will threaten, if not to crash, then at least to generate less prosperity. 'Sink or swim' is the motto. So if we swim, our chances of a total crash fall, because with such a high degree of interaction and connectivity there is a great likelihood that enough people will play the game and enough variability in the range of offers will develop, and this will create new attractions. But at the same time, our chances of experiencing great and lasting booms fall. In a real-time world, phases of boom and recession get shorter and shorter until they are barely recognizable.

It is of course exciting to see that, in this process, all fixed values become fluid values. The ultimate parameter for evaluations, for ratings, for appreciation, for categorization, but also for motivation, is money or, in a real-time world, price. Money is abstract and can react flexibly to complexity and dynamic movement. Money has no other point of reference but itself. Our last refuge is the security offered by the current price. We are all equal in the face of money or of the real-time price. 'Money doesn't rule democracy; money is democracy,' says a US expert on financial markets, and he is not entirely wrong. Markets are primarily relevant as time markets that take advantage of time structures, and real markets mimic financial markets.

The rules of the financial markets lead to less down-to-earth behaviour and much less sustainable results than we have become accustomed to on the real markets. While even during a boom the real markets were much more resistant to euphoria and over-evaluation, the financial markets, driven by human weakness, push a 'paper growth'. As it is always 'only' about paper and the exchange of paper values – 'paper entrepreneurialism', as Robert B Reich calls it[2] – real money degenerates into play money. Like the ball in a game of roulette, it is thrown into the wheel to realize profits. Thus, aggressive accounting and aggressive spending are interdependent. If you spend aggressively on one hand, you have to do some aggressive accounting on the other to make up for it. And that is precisely what the financial institutions did in the boom years. In the realm of the abstract and speculative, mechanisms that place a high value on a sensible degree of comprehensibility in the real world of the economy fail. However, let us not be naïve about this: paper entrepreneurialism would not be an entirely bad thing if only it did not generate a susceptibility to illusions and if it were more productive. But instead of generating technological or institutional innovation, it creates innovation by means of creative accounting, tax deferral, financial management or litigation.[3] All these are forms of paper innovation that keep legal and moral systems flexible. Their only relevance for our subject here is that this way of thinking, which dominates the financial markets, is now also beginning to dominate the real markets.

There is a predominant focus on price. Products or services are not relevant in themselves, only their tradability. The utilization value or experience value are no longer dominant, only tradability. So yield management is a trend that will gain even more ground in the years to come, and dynamic pricing is its weapon. As we have seen by looking at the travel sector (hotels, airlines), yield management means that the decisive factor for customers is the best, ie the lowest, price. What was originally developed as a pure pricing instrument is now perceived by customers as a discount instrument.

This means that the tendency is for prices and products or services not to be as firmly linked as they were. Uniform prices are gradually becoming less important, for the plain and simple reason that in a dynamic and complex economy they are a less-than-optimum means to ensure profits. Factors that are fixed and not subject to constant fluctuation may be easier to handle – the uniform price of the products on the retailer's shelves – but that is of less and less interest today. In this way, increased price

competence becomes vital for success. New forms of differentiation and discrimination gain in importance more when markets
and products are mature or oversaturated when judged by other
criteria. Nowadays, pricing systems have clearly defined preconditions and goals. They must:

- encourage customers to consume more;
- make it more difficult for customers to swap to other suppliers; and
- reduce comparability of prices.

Wherever we see the megatrend towards more transparency,
comparability and consumer empowerment, we will immediately
see the countertrend towards obfuscation, segregation and a
return to monopolistic conditions. Here, too, the financial
markets have a lot to teach us. On the real markets, there is no
better example than that of the airlines. The goal for the
supplier is optimum profit with fluctuating prices that are
adjusted in real time according to supply and demand. Price
control is exercised by means of an array of key data, which are
readily available. This is an attempt to realize as much profit as
possible with the help of customer- and product-specific data
and knowledge of discounts, margins, process costs etc. The aim
is to bind customers to a system in which they are encouraged to
buy again and again and that gives them the feeling they are
getting a good deal. For preference, customers are sold individu-
alized 'tailor-made' packages that make it impossible for them to
make direct price comparisons. In other words, customers have
to decide how much the product is worth to them. Otherwise,
they will become increasingly dependent on a supplier until they
reach a point where they no longer feel comfortable with the
situation. Customers have to be aware at all times what their
switching costs are: do I still have a choice, or am I heading
towards a situation in which I have no alternatives, caught up in

a closed system because I am offered more and more additional incentives (discounts, bonus miles, VIP treatment etc)? As soon as the switching costs become too high, something has gone wrong. This situation has to be avoided at all costs to prevent frustration and dissatisfaction.

However, this also leads to a fluid evaluation of products and services. There are no 'fixed' values any more. Let us make a few banal comparisons. Why is a pair of trainers marked down in a sale still three times more expensive than a flight from London to Milan? Why is a flight from Berlin to Zurich cheaper than the taxi fare from the airport into town? Why is a Casio calculator cheaper than a small packet of own-brand cornflakes? There are some even more striking examples. The refill cartridges for my HP printer cost more than the printer itself did. The sausages on the barbecue are more expensive than the barbecue itself. There has been a shift in relative values here. The value of products and services, the point at which values are generated in the added-value chain, has become more diffuse and more volatile.

Only a few years ago, every time a new half-price or even quarter-price offer was announced, customers would wonder: how do they do it? Does it make commercial sense? Or are their 'normal' prices too high? Today, consumer consciousness is so well developed that we no longer ask these questions. You get used to being offered low prices – though sometimes you have to look for them. In the age of global sourcing, customers are better informed than ever before and potentially more critical. But here, too, there is a contradiction. A customer who buys a pile of five T-shirts for 5 euros no longer asks where they came from and how they were manufactured. A low price is always good. And the fact that the very same customer is willing to buy organic produce and health food now and again to soothe his or her conscience just confirms the everyday schizophrenia of our shopping habits. We see no relationship any more between the costs of producing a product and its selling price. The customer has forgotten that there was ever a link between the two. The megatrends *individualization*, *flexibilization* and *economization* have permeated our consciousness, and each of the three reinforces the other two.[4] They continue to affect us and are achieving their full potential in the Age of Cheap.

Individualization, which in its extreme form becomes hyperindividualism[5] – there are no wishes that could not be expressed legitimately and satisfied in the form of a product or a service. Individualization is so strong a trend that it is becoming a farce. The best example is human relationships. There has been no better example of how to turn a human desire into a product and market it than our desire to meet other people. And hardly any other market has such promising growth rates. Speed dating is now available in almost every city, satisfying the demand for getting to know as many people as possible within a controlled framework, with a brief and non-committal encounter where I can take a look at the other person, sound the person out with a little small talk and then decide whether I want to take it any further. This phase can take the form of anything from a one-minute to an eight-minute date. If I find the other person OK and I want to go on to the next round, I say so. If I don't like the person, I break off the date and never have to see him or her again. I can register under appropriate names like HurryDate, FastDate, 8minute Dating or Speed Dating. One particularly speedy dater is Steve Lee, a hedge-fund manager from Manhattan. A qualified financial specialist, he had 2,500 speed dates, each lasting three minutes, in the space of 16 months. Each date cost $1.45. The speed dates then led to more than 100 real dates that lasted longer than one cup of coffee. It seems that Steve Lee finally got lucky and has even found someone he plans to marry. The striking thing is that these dating sessions are organized in the same way as a project is managed or a business plan implemented. The important question is: how many people can I get to know in what period of time, and how much will I have to invest? Efficiency, effectiveness and price are the decisive factors. Cheap is good. Speed dating, cheap death and cheap porn[6] have the same mindset, and the same type of manager is behind them all.

The desire to have children is almost as ubiquitous as the desire to find a partner. And the creativity with which people conduct a search to get just the child they want is also boundless. The US lesbian couple Sharon Duchesneau and Candy McCullough, from Bethesda in Maryland, were both born deaf. Their greatest wish was a child who was also deaf. Nowadays, it's easy to find a sperm donor, for example at mannotincluded.com, a website that offers 'Private fertility – for lesbians and single women'. After drawing a blank there, the two women found a sperm donor in the family of some friends, a family whose members were all deaf and had been deaf for five generations due to a genetic condition. So baby Gauvin McCullough was born. He was born deaf, but developed minimal hearing in one ear after a few months. The couple intend to let Gauvin himself decide later whether he wants a hearing aid or not.[7] Their reasons for wanting a deaf baby are hyperindividualistic: deafness is not an illness that has to be cured but a cultural identity one assumes. They want the baby to have the same experiences and feelings its parents had. This is a very good example of how legal limits can be interpreted in a highly individualistic manner. You can justify anything in this way. The law is flexible, just as flexible as human expectations.

Another example that can be mentioned here is that of a Dutch student from Haarlem – even though this is more a media-interest story and one that touches more on aesthetic values – who decided to enter into a solo marriage: the young lady married herself. Thirty-year-old Jennifer Hoes published the banns and turned up at the register office before registrar Ruud Grondel wearing the obligatory wedding dress. Even though such an act could not be legalized, it shows how the logic can be taken to extremes. Jennifer gave the following reason for her decision: 'We live in a "Me" society. Hence it is logical that one promises to be faithful to oneself.' The bride's refusal to become emotionally dependent on anyone else and her resolve to be true to no one but herself is perhaps one that many women will understand. What we can see here, however, is a seamless transition from hyperindividualism to hyper-democracy. Hyper-democracy means that there is no value that does not have a legitimate claim to political realization. And that, of course, makes things immeasurably complex and dynamic. It means that there is no subject too absurd to appear on the agendas of parliaments and executive organs. We can already see today that the topics under public discussion are becoming more and more banal and self-centred. Democracy would become the art of consciously losing ourselves in the banal and also possessing the patience to see it through. In fact, that is a tremendous achievement, and one we could be proud of politically. The triumph of the banal – for example, *Big Brother*. Because individualism has mutated to hyperindividualism, I no longer know how to put on my pyjamas. Or whether men should really sit down to urinate and not stand. And because I lack these everyday certainties, because they are no longer common knowledge, because everyone can do it their own way and is supposed to do it their own way, I can learn to compensate indirectly for my ignorance with an entertainment format like *Big Brother*.

We have already begun to describe the transition from flexibilization to hyperflexibilization. If there are no legitimate limits to individualization any more, the volatility of values also becomes unlimited and becomes a parody of itself. In the last few years, we have seen a steady increase in pragmatism, both in corporate life and in the world of politics. There are no discussions about which direction to take or basic issues any more. On the one hand, that is great and a marvellous achievement. No one seriously wants a return to the old ideologies. But on the other hand, we have also lost the ability to think deeply about ideas or the direction we want to take. Today, no politician can recognize ideo-political correlations, think in a connected manner or lay down broad lines. Everyday pragmatism dominates. This way today, that way tomorrow, and everyone has forgotten what happened yesterday anyway. This could be seen as a cause for regret, but the advantage is that here, too, we can see the opinion markets at work. What applies to the real markets also applies to the opinion markets: real markets will mimic financial markets. And so it is no coincidence that instant polling has become the national sport in many of the richer nations. It is guaranteed to attract attention and ensures high TV ratings. I want to know, every minute and in real time, where my favourite politician stands in people's opinion. The higher his or her rating, the more popular the politician is and the more he or she is worth. Hyperflexibilization brings hyper-pragmatism and hyper-democracy.

But in a connected world, hyper-pragmatism also means hyper-econo-mization. What is worth what? Prices remain the most important parameter and anchor. So in a hyper-democratic economy and society, 'cheap' will win the day. It is the common denominator that everyone understands. And it brings the promise of goods for everyone. Rich nations often underestimate the motivation of other nations – everyone wants their cut. The bulldozer rolls on relentlessly. The Age of Cheap is likely to occupy us for many years to come. And we will have to get used to a 'new sobriety' in handling subjects and problems. No less a man than Karl Marx described it inimitably in his *Communist Manifesto*.[8] If the price is right, OK, but if the price is wrong, it's a no-go.

In the Western world today, we have a standard of living Karl Marx could never have dreamed of. In this respect, his proletarian prognoses turned out to be far too pessimistic. His ideal of a classless society has long been understood and implemented mentally. And in addition, we have much more insight and 150 years' more experience than Marx when he wrote his *Communist Manifesto*. But in their basic tendency, most of his statements were undeniably true. And so the *Manifesto* is worth reading even today. It is a worthy substitute for 99 per cent of the 'new' social and economic literature on the market, not to mention the literature on management.

> It is more likely that the globalization of capitalism will result in the banalities of an ever-increasing, worldwide consumerist culture. Recall that Athens ceased to be a world power around 400 B.C., yet for the next 300 years Greek culture was the culture of the world. The Age of European Exposition ended in mid-20th century: the Age of American Markets – Yankee imperialism – is just starting to gather force.[9]

Maybe Wal-Mart will collapse under its own weight when, in the foreseeable future, its turnover passes the $1 trillion mark and its workforce of 6 million is no longer manageable. Then, indeed, we would be faced with a completely new situation. But then again, perhaps not, and we will all become Wal-Mart.

> Wal-Mart is the logical end point and the future of the economy in a society whose pre-eminent value is getting the best deal.
>
> Robert B Reich, former Labor Secretary and Professor of Social and Economic Policy, Brandeis University

Notes

[1]   See GDI-Impuls 1.03, which is dedicated to the subject of 'Questions of price', especially the articles by Georg Wübker and Hermann Simon, 'Wege aus der Preiskriegsfalle: Innovative Pricing-Strategien sind der Gewinntreiber schlechthin', pp 36–43, and Mark Ritson, Mark Zbaracki *et al*, 'Pricing als strategische Ressource', pp 16–22.

[2]   Robert B Reich (1983) *The Next American Frontier*, New York Times Books, New York.

3 See Charles W Mulford and Eugene E Comiskey (2002) *The Financial Numbers Game: Detecting creative accounting practices*, John Wiley, New York. This book, published before the Enron scandal, highlights all the different techniques and tactics employed, from aggressive accounting, earnings management, income smoothing and fraudulent financial reporting to creative accounting practices.

4 See David Bosshart and Karin Frick (2003) 'Megatrends basic: 7 megatrends und gegentrends', GDI study.

5 The term 'hyperindividualisme' was coined in the French discussion and has been used frequently in a socio-scientific context.

6 See Chapter 1.

7 See http://news.bbc.co.uk/1/hi/health/1916462.stm.

8 See the *Communist Party Manifesto*, published in London in 1848, quoted from Marx/Engels (1980) *Werke*, Vol 4, Dietz Verlag, Berlin, pp 459–93, in particular with reference to easier communication, 'cash payment', the compulsion for all to participate, the relief of all misery etc.

9 James B Twitchell (2000) 'In praise of consumerism', *Reason*, August/September.

8 The next chapter

The new normality in globalizing markets

We are all becoming part of a contradictory global order. Things we can delay politically, things that confront us with organizational difficulties, and processes that we find difficult to organize are driven forward faster and faster by the forces of technology and are implemented in economic life in the form of new business models. This means that we live in an age where the greatest challenge is the synchronization of speed. Technologically, we are already travelling in supersonic planes, economically we are driving a Porsche, socially we reach at most the speed of a cyclist, and politically we are moving only at snail's pace. The winners in our world are able to use these different speeds for their own purposes – as clever discounters have demonstrated in recent years. Whatever the new world order looks like, from an economic point of view, price and the watchword 'cheap' will play a dominant role in coming years. Prices are the accelerators of development, and the much discussed sharper polarization between premium and discount segments continues at unbroken speed.

The fact that the German edition of this book sold out so quickly can be taken as an indication that it is an accurate representation of the trends at work in our society. Feedback from readers has been excellent, encouraging and confirming. The right subject at the right moment. The question I am asked again and again is: 'In your personal opinion, is "cheap" good or bad?' There is of course no clear answer to that, only one that is paradoxical. On the one hand, we have the many advantages for customers and can look forward to many innovative projects. On the other, we have to accept that there will be a shift in the distribution of orders, and of income and wealth. We have to learn to live with paradox and learn how to make wise decisions with very little time for reflection. This is not an easy task for us Old Europeans. So far, time has for us been a resource in (almost) endless supply. However, now we have to decide what we want, politically, economically and socially. And if we fail to make a decision, the markets will decide for us.

Take Austria as an example. With the expansion of the European Union, it has acquired new neighbours overnight: the Czech Republic, Slovenia, Slovakia and Hungary. This immediately triggers a debate about relative advantages. Who can do what and make what at a better price? Insurance premiums for car insurance policy holders in Vienna can be cut by 30 per cent. Great news for the customers! This is possible because damaged cars can be transported by truck to Bratislava, 60 kilometres away, where repairs can be carried out to the same standards and at a fraction of the cost. Good news for repair shops in Bratislava. For them, this means new business and plenty of work. At the same time, this is a challenge for repair shops in Vienna. Such developments encourage innovation, and that is good. But on the other hand, national economies that have had little experience with competition are unable to react in time, let alone develop proactive strategies.

It is no coincidence that pricing is one of the most popular subjects for lectures and workshops. Retailers and more and more manufacturers have to learn to abandon discounts and campaigns and elevate pricing to the level of a strategic tool. It will be necessary to replace hectic operational activity with strategic skill in order to survive the coming years and become stronger in the process, because customers are going to be looking at goods and services through an even finer filter. Who has a better price image but at the same time offers high quality and a high degree of customer orientation?

- 'I'm cheap' – that is the basis for Wal-Mart's claim: EDLP – every day low prices or even best price. Today, customers have come to expect a good price and a good price–performance ratio, in other words so-called value retailing. And customer expectations are not likely to fall, whether the economic situation improves or not.
- 'I'm not expensive' – this is the solution now favoured by even the famous top-brand and premium-brand retailers.
- 'I'm cheaper than the company that boasts that it's the cheapest' – this is the message we get from the most aggressive suppliers, for example Lidl. And what is true of the discounters also applies to the hypermarkets: Leclerc in France has managed to establish for itself a more playful image than that of its most important rivals, who are trying to improve their price image.
- 'I have the cheapest branded goods' – this is another passionate battle cry in the ever-keener struggle between retailers' own brands and manufacturers' brands. If Carrefour is unsuccessful in establishing for itself a better price image than Leclerc, it will try to succeed with its own brands: 'Our own brands are the cheapest', they will cry. And of course the big suppliers, for example Pick Pay in Switzerland, also try to

get the message across that they stock the cheapest manufacturers' brands. Hofer (Aldi) customers in Austria go to the market leaders Billa and Spar, not in search of cheap own brands but cheap manufacturers' brands.

- 'I'm often very cheap' – finally, this is the battle cry of all those who have a guilty conscience because their price image is not good. They launch large-scale drives and come up with new ideas all the time to attract more customers with price cuts and thus break the hold of the reference price.

Anyone who fails to recognize that price is a strategic instrument is probably doomed to launch continued attempts to attract more customers – and is in danger of walking into a lethal trap. If they blur their image and fail to establish a profile as suppliers of attractively priced goods, suppliers of quality goods or suppliers of services, sooner or later they will run into almost insurmountable problems. If you advertise via prices, consumers see you and judge you as a supplier of low-price goods. If you present yourself as a provider of quality goods or services, you have to communicate prices in a more differentiated manner. This is likely to be a point at which divergence will become more and more pronounced in the coming years:

- Pricing as an instrument to generate higher customer frequency, as we have seen it demonstrated by the discounters. The goal is to generate a turnover hike by tempting more customers into the store. It is logical and consistent that, in order to do so, it is more and more common to adopt methods borrowed from the entertainment sector. Coop's Pfannentrophy in Switzerland is a good example.
- Pricing as an instrument to generate customer loyalty, as we would expect in the case of full-range suppliers and service providers.

Even in the premium sector, there will be a more differentiated perception of price. Few suppliers can afford to neglect the question of price altogether. Customer sensitivity is increasing. We compare everything with everything else and are only prepared to spend a lot of money where we perceive an added personal value. In a world of increasingly global competition, of easy access to information, of improved communication and an increasing supply overhang, on many levels we are moving towards a world in which 'cheap' is the norm:

- We spend money more consciously (overspend when there is a real added value perceived, underspend on everyday requirements with no added value, ie the mundane goods and services we require to satisfy our basic needs).
- Different customers have different price profiles. This doesn't make the development any easier, but a lot more interesting.
- Every product group or every brand has its own price profile. This also contributes to the increasing complexity of markets, particularly in Old Europe. No other region in the world can boast such demanding, critical and well-informed customers. With ageing populations, it is going to become more of a challenge to earn money here.
- The predictability and planning of consumer behaviour are not increasing. The so-called rational type (the customer who plans purchases or makes considered choices after comparing products) and the so-called emotional type (the customer who mainly buys in bulk and on impulse) are increasingly one and the same person. The only insight that still holds true is that women tend to be more rational buyers as they are better informed, while men tend to be emotional shoppers because they are mainly amateurs at the game of shopping.

So we are approaching an age where, thanks to the Age of Cheap, we are learning a new normality. On the one hand, this 'new normality' means increasing price consciousness. An insecure economic climate and fewer certainties with respect to our own future render a certain basic caution advisable. It is clear that this in itself can lead to paradox and paradoxical behaviour – we buy too much of things we don't need just because the price is low at the moment and are too afraid to take even reasonable risks.

On the other hand, increasing price consciousness means a greater need for simplicity. We only feel that we decide our own fate, have everything under control and are not simply being steamrollered by things if we can make quick, uncomplicated decisions. Too much complexity, too many products on offer and too much information produce customer confusion – it doesn't make us inclined to buy more. These are a few of the main reasons why discounting as a business model – even if, as is the case in Germany, the discounters will soon be jostling for position among themselves – can still be a pioneering example.

And lastly, more than ever before, customers need an emotional bond – they need to feel connected. The price is the most important instrument. But anyone who uses this instrument will in the end be forced to come up with something new at ever-shorter intervals. No other instrument is perceived with such acuity by the customer as the price. And no other instrument is more exciting when it is wielded as a weapon.

Index